Praise for *Going*

'For most of us, "viral content" has become the modern day Holy Grail - a nearly mythological thing that's always just outside of our grasp. Finally, here's a book that reveals the secrets about how to make the myth a reality. I can't wait to put these ideas into action.'

Steve Farber, author, *The Radical Leap, The Radical Edge* **and** *Greater Than Yourself*

'One does not go viral, one has to read Brent's book first to understand the dynamics of becoming worthy of sharing.'

Brian Solis, author, *X: The Experience When Business Meets Design*

'There will always be a degree of unpredictability in any attempts to create viral video, but Brent's work will help you improve your odds substantially.'

Rory Sutherland, Vice Chairman, Ogilvy & Mather

'A fascinating deep dive into what drives us to share.'

Pamela Meyer, CEO, Calibrate and top 20 TED speaker

GOING VIRAL

PEARSON

At Pearson, we believe in learning – all kinds of learning for all kinds of people. Whether it's at home, in the classroom or in the workplace, learning is the key to improving our life chances.

That's why we're working with leading authors to bring you the latest thinking and best practices, so you can get better at the things that are important to you. You can learn on the page or on the move, and with content that's always crafted to help you understand quickly and apply what you've learned.

If you want to upgrade your personal skills or accelerate your career, become a more effective leader or more powerful communicator, discover new opportunities or simply find more inspiration, we can help you make progress in your work and life.

Pearson is the world's leading learning company. Our portfolio includes the Financial Times and our education business, Pearson International.

Every day our work helps learning flourish, and wherever learning flourishes, so do people.

To learn more, please visit us at **www.pearson.com/uk**

Going Viral

The 9 secrets of irresistible marketing

BRENT COKER

Harlow, England • London • New York • Boston • San Francisco • Toronto • Sydney • Auckland • Singapore • Hong Kong
Tokyo • Seoul • Taipei • New Delhi • Cape Town • São Paulo • Mexico City • Madrid • Amsterdam • Munich • Paris • Milan

PEARSON EDUCATION LIMITED
Edinburgh Gate
Harlow CM20 2JE
United Kingdom
Tel: +44 (0)1279 623623
Web: **www.pearson.com/uk**

First edition published 2016 (print and electronic)

ISBN: 978-1-292-08792-4 (print)
     978-1-292-08794-8 (PDF)
     978-1-292-08795-5 (ePub)

British Library Cataloguing-in-Publication Data
A catalogue record for the print edition is available from the British Library

Library of Congress Cataloging-in-Publication Data
Names: Coker, Brent, author.
Title: Going viral: the 9 secrets of irresistible marketing / Brent Coker.
Description: First edition. | Harlow, England; New York: Pearson, 2016. |
   Includes index.
Identifiers: LCCN 2015041954 | ISBN 9781292087924 (pbk.)
Subjects: LCSH: Marketing—Social aspects. | Internet marketing.
Classification: LCC HF5415 .C5426 2016 | DDC 658.8—dc23
LC record available at http://lccn.loc.gov/2015041954

10 9 8 7 6 5 4 3 2 1
20 19 18 17 16

Cover design by Two Associates

Print edition typeset in 9.5 pt and ITC Giovanni Std by SPi Global
Printed in Great Britain by Henry Ling Ltd, at the Dorset Press, Dorchester, Dorset

NOTE THAT ANY PAGE CROSS REFERENCES REFER TO THE PRINT EDITION

For Mitsue

Contents

About the author

Brent Coker woke up one day to find his research on workplace internet leisure browsing had gone viral. Since then, he has been researching why ideas spread and what causes people to share. He has a PhD in online consumer psychology, and is developer of the bump algorithm that predicts the spread of memes and video ads. Coker has appeared on CNN, Fox News Business and MSNBC, to name a few. He lives in Melbourne, Australia, where in his spare time he enjoys cycling (for fitness) and motorcycling (for fun).

Publisher's acknowledgements

We are grateful to the following for permission to reproduce copyright material:

Photo on page 5 © ZUMA Press, Inc./ Alamy Stock Photo; photo on page 18 © Catchlight Visual Services/ Alamy Stock Photo; photo on page 33 © Veronica Louro/ 123rf.com; photo on page 55 © Ryan Ladbrook/ Shutterstock.com; photo on page 65 © Andrew Spiers/ Alamy Stock Photo; photo on page 88 © 123rf.com; photo on page 90 © Ian Dagnall/ Alamy Stock Photo.

Introduction

Soon after graduating from my PhD in internet consumer psychology, I began to plan my next big project. I had just spent three years of my life working on my thesis, and I couldn't wait to start afresh on something new. It was 2007. YouTube was just starting to become popular, and word was getting around about something called 'social media' and a new website called 'Facebook'. More people were organising their lives on the internet than ever before – banking, shopping, planning, and now social. The internet was now firmly engrained into society, and I was excited to begin my career studying its effects on people.

I noticed news stories beginning to appear about employers who were blocking external internet access during work hours. Apparently many organisations viewed the internet as a threat to productivity, and they were suspicious that their employees were using it for personal reasons when they should have been working. I found the idea of companies losing productivity because of the internet intriguing, and so I decided to see if I could measure how much productivity was actually being lost.

My first challenge was figuring out how to measure national productivity, since I wanted to correlate internet use in the workplace with the productivity of the nation. My research training up to that point was in behavioural science and I had few clues about measuring such things, so I called a friend of mine who was an economist. Sergey was a talented economist from Moscow, and I thought that if anyone had the answer it would be him. I arranged to meet Sergey for coffee.

We met at a local café. I remember he paused for quite some time when I explained to him what I was trying to do. After considerable thought he replied in his thick Muscovite accent: 'Not possible!' According to Sergey, attempts at measuring national productivity as a function of internet use would likely give unreliable results.

I went back to my office to rethink what I was trying to do, and before the end of the day I had a new plan. I decided instead to measure productivity at the firm level, knowing that if I studied enough firms I'd be able to generalise the results. I began reading past research on firm productivity, and as I got further into it I came to an unexpected realisation. The more I read, the more I began to suspect that perhaps my hypothesis about productivity being *lost* as a result of using the internet for personal reasons, might be wrong. Several studies suggested that mini-breaks in the workplace should *improve* overall productivity. Other studies suggested that productivity and loyalty were lower for workers who were inhibited from being able to organise their lives while at work. Against my initial assumption, it was beginning to look like workers who could access external internet sites should have *higher* productivity than those who couldn't.

Excited with my new hypothesis, I hurried to collect the data I needed. I gathered data from a large sample of office workers across a variety of industries, and began my analysis. Sure enough, the data suggested that those who were able to use the internet freely in the workplace were more productive than those who had their outside internet access blocked.

I was pretty excited about my findings, and my university was keen to have the results of my study sent to some local reporters. David Scott, the university media manager, drafted a quick news release and sent it out. 'Make sure you're available tomorrow morning in case anyone wants to run a story on it', he told me. One local paper in particular – *mX News*, the free paper available at inner city tram stops – was showing some interest. I was flattered.

I woke up the next morning to my phone ringing. It was David. 'Brent! Where have you been!?' He exclaimed in an excited voice. 'I've been trying to get in contact with you – check your emails!' I opened my computer – I had over 4000 new emails from people I had never heard of, and they were still loading. Many were reporters requesting an interview, others were office workers thanking me for my study, people with questions, and academics congratulating me. 'David what's happened?' I asked, surprised and at the same time a little panicked. 'Your study is in the *New York Times* and it's trending on Twitter!' he exclaimed. I sat back in my chair in disbelief.

For the next few days my phone didn't stop ringing. I gave radio station and media interviews from the USA to Europe, and fielded what seemed like a never-ending barrage of emails. The press were reporting that a new study had found that surfing the internet at work was good for productivity.

For some reason people couldn't stop talking about it. The results of my 'Freedom to surf' study had gone viral.

I had my 15 minutes of fame as they say. But what really intrigued me about what had happened was why my story had spread so wide and far, and so quickly. And so began my next research interest: why things go viral. This book is an account of what I've learned.

Going viral

Important advances in medicine or agricultural improvements to food production bring us closer to reducing the pain and suffering in this world. No one would argue that this information isn't important for mankind's wellbeing. Yet most people would rather talk about whether a dress is blue-and-black or white-and-gold, than how much more yield a new strain of rice is able to produce. I bet there were probably a hundred more important academic studies released the same time as mine – incremental advances in science that might eventually solve some serious problems in the world. In comparison, my study was probably quite trivial. But everyone wanted to talk about it.

And herein lies the first lesson when it comes to going viral. It's not the importance of the message that makes it spread, but rather the value of sharing. All viral content has one thing in common – it motivates people to share. Incremental advances in science, though quite important, won't go viral if people aren't motivated to share them with others.

Behind people's motives to share is a multifaceted and complex set of psychological routines that defines when, how and why people behave the way they do. If something is interesting, people will tell others about it. That seems to be obvious. But what is 'interesting', and how does it make people share? If it were simple then we wouldn't continue to see failed advertising campaigns, brands that fail to take off, or good ideas that never spread. To understand why things go viral we have to dig deep, not just defining what is interesting, but how information and the media affect people in powerful and predictable ways. Viral marketing is not about getting people to take notice, it's about how to affect people in a meaningful and memorable way.

The ideas in this book span leading-edge research from such diverse fields as psychology, mathematics and economics. *Going Viral* doesn't just explain why things go viral, but it also gives an insight into, and instruction on, the techniques needed to make something go viral.

The explanation and prediction of viral success are described in nine chapters:

▶ **Chapter 1: The power of share.** What motivates people to share content with others? Viral marketing requires a different mindset to classical marketing. In this chapter I explain how exchange in value motivates sharing behaviour. You'll learn the secret of what motivates people to share, and how content can be designed to activate these motives.

▶ **Chapter 2: Self-enhancement.** What are the social factors that influence people's decisions to share? In this chapter I explain how the core values of people's membership in society, and their attempts to make an impression and seek approval from others, influence their decisions to share. You'll learn the secret of how to craft shareable content through understanding the psychology of your target audience.

▶ **Chapter 3: Emotion.** How does emotion cause people to share? In this chapter I discuss the importance of emotion, why emotion causes sharing behaviour, and how to evoke an emotional response. You'll learn the secret of how to generate strong emotions, and how to transfer the emotions most effectively.

▶ **Chapter 4: Anticipation.** How can you create a physiological response? In this chapter I discuss the curious properties of anticipation, how sharing is linked to a biological response mechanism, and how mental attentiveness causes people to share. You'll learn the secrets of how to create a physiological response that makes memorable content shareable.

▶ **Chapter 5: Affinity.** How do people's feelings influence their decisions to share? In this chapter I discuss the role of affinity in influencing viral spread. Affinity is more than just relevance, it's a feeling of warmth and deep appreciation. In this chapter you'll learn the secrets behind the power of affinity.

▶ **Chapter 6: Justice.** What causes people to support something and want it to win? In this chapter I discuss the role of justice and how people have a strong desire to support effort over ability. You'll learn the secrets of how to earn underdog support through creating an unfair disadvantage, and how people's sense of justice influences their motives to share.

▶ **Chapter 7: Herding.** How do you release your shareable content into the wild? In this chapter I guide you through the intricacies of seeding your content to give it the best chances of spreading in the early stages. You'll learn the secrets of how to choose which networks to seed to, how to choose the correct people, and the usefulness of social proof.

▶ **Chapter 8: Groups.** How can you add fuel to the fire? In this chapter I introduce the fundamentals of group-based sharing, and how to generate viral buzz to aid the spread of your shareable content. You'll learn the secret of how to design your content for group-based sharing, and how contentiousness and loyalty drive viral buzz.

▶ **Chapter 9: Bump.** What's the best way to add a brand to shareable content? In this final chapter I discuss the options available for adding a brand to your content, and the power of storytelling. You'll learn the secrets of the bump framework, and how to structure a branded video ad to maximise emotional transfer and sharing.

In these nine chapters I've summarised research that has studied the antecedents leading to the viral spread of information across diverse fields of science. I've used real-life examples and tales of inspiration to exemplify how to put the nine secrets into practice. The secrets behind viral success shouldn't be hidden in advanced formulas, or buried in obscure journals. I believe they should be accessible to everyone.

I wrote this book for anyone yearning to know the secrets behind the world's most viral ideas, and for those who want to create a message that people can't resist sharing. When your idea goes viral it's a magical shortcut to the top of the mountain, bypassing all the pitfalls, the pain, and the hurt of trying to 'make it'. The biggest myth about going viral is that it's a function of randomness. That an idea somehow got lucky. By the time you finish this book, you'll understand why it's not random, and why you don't need to be lucky to get your message spread wide and far. You *can* influence your own success. Whether you're a small business owner, an advertising exec, or a person on the street who has a message that needs to be shared, this book is for you.

A different mindset

In 2013 I travelled to São Paulo in Brazil to present at a conference. Sitting in the taxi on my way from the airport to the hotel, I gazed out the window at the scenery flying by. This was my first time in South America, and I couldn't wait to explore the city. But I soon developed a feeling of uneasiness. Something was just not right, and I couldn't put my finger on it. Then almost at the hotel it struck me. My troubled feelings were caused by something missing in the scenery. Curiously, there was no advertising in São Paulo.

I was so used to seeing billboards, placards, and branded signs dotted around that my mind had registered an abnormality. Surely São Paulo must have marketing, I thought to myself. What was going on? Soon after arriving at my hotel and settling in, I asked someone why there was no advertising outside. Their answer surprised me. São Paulo banned outdoor advertising in 2006 – the first city in the world to do so. For *Paulistanos* (people from São Paulo), outdoor advertising was viewed as a form of pollution.

Being a marketer, the fact that the people around me thought advertising was a form of pollution made me feel a little awkward, but at the same time I was quietly impressed. Other nations might view São Paulo's stance on outdoor advertising as a bit extreme, but I don't think the attitudes held by Paulistanos are actually all that unusual. Each day most of us are exposed to dozens, sometimes hundreds, of advertising messages, but do we really want that? Most of us have learned to live with advertisements, and even block them out. This has been the challenge for marketers for decades: how to get noticed among the noise of all the other brands vying to get people's attention.

The antithesis to viral marketing is to create controversy. The theory is that if people are shocked, then they'll at least take notice. But there's a fundamental problem with using controversy to get noticed. Creating controversy relies on creating an emotional response using negative emotions such as disgust, grief, or occasionally fear. These are not pleasant emotions, and generally people will try to avoid feeling them. A picture of a young boy suffocating with a plastic bag over his head, or the Pope kissing a Muslim leader on the lips (both actual advertisements) might create intrigue and interest, but they create few reasons to share. For this reason, these types of advertising strategies rarely go viral. People will share a joke with others quite readily, because it makes other people happy, but it's difficult to imagine why someone would want to bring other people down by sharing advertisements designed to shock.

In the days before the internet, people were less connected. Even to this day, outside of the internet people really only have around three close friends. On the internet life is different – nowadays the average Facebook user has over 300 friends. The internet is a machine that enables rapid information sharing in the shortest time possible, between hundreds and thousands of people at the same time. It's the ideal catalyst for creating a viral. But although we're connected to more people than ever before, we're not close to them all. We'll interact with a subset of the people in our networks regularly, but most of them we won't. We'll readily share something amusing with them all, but we'll think twice about sharing something that might put our character into question. Social media is like a town square – normal people don't go there to shock or dismay, they go there to be social. People care about what other people think, and this influences what they decide to share.

The more closely you know someone, the more likely it is that you'll share something negative. There is a tendency for people to share sad, fearful or disgusting experiences with people they're close to, as a way to come to terms with them. But rarely will people share negative experiences with people they don't know so well.

Controversial advertising doesn't go viral because it involves negative emotions, and people are hesitant to evoke negative emotions with people who aren't close to them. The internet has increased sharing, but at the same time the dynamics of what is shared has changed. People are more selective about what they share, and their reasons for sharing have become more refined.

This book requires a different mindset. It's not about creating controversy or getting noticed above the noise. It's about creating something of value – something that people will be glad to experience, and share with others.

CHAPTER ONE

The power of share

In 2010 I was sitting at my desk putting together some notes for a night class I was scheduled to teach, when I got a phone call. The woman calling introduced herself as Cheryl, and explained that she was the director of a boutique advertising agency in Sydney, Australia. Her voice was rushed and forceful, like she was stressed. She explained she had heard I was doing research into viral movies, and wanted some advice. I was flattered she called me, and curious.

We chatted for about five minutes, where after some small talk and pleasantries she explained her predicament. She told me her agency had recently taken on a client who wanted to launch a new brand of underwear. Her brief was to produce an advertisement for the internet that needed to 'go viral'. The problem was that the advertisement wasn't creating buzz – after several months it had barely 400 views, and the client wanted answers.

Cheryl was understandably desperate, and wanted to find out if anything could be done to fix it. To make it go viral. Before the phone call ended I promised Cheryl I would take a look at the campaign, though secretly suspecting that it would be unlikely anything could be fixed.

I set aside my class preparation, and clicked on the link she sent me. It was a 'personalised story' type advertisement, a technique I had seen before. How this technique works is that the viewer is first asked to upload a photo of themselves that is eventually included in the story. The aim is to surprise the viewer who isn't expecting to become part of the story. I uploaded a photo of myself, selected male for my gender, and sat back and watched.

The movie began with a pan of a half-lit retro-fitted studio apartment. The camera focussed, and a woman appeared from the shadows of the apartment wearing lingerie. She glided past a coffee table, pausing to pick up a magazine, and headed towards her bed. She lay on the bed and opened the magazine, snapping through a few pages before pausing on one with intent. The camera zoomed in on the page to show a muscular tanned male posing in a G-string. The camera zoomed in more to reveal the face – it was me!

Then things got steamy – as the women glared at the picture she began to caress herself, and ... I flashed back to my phone conversation with Cheryl, and felt uncomfortable.

It was obvious to me why the ad hadn't gone viral. The problem wasn't the quality of the production – clearly a lot of effort and expense had gone into it. Where it went wrong was that it assumed that sex sells. Or more precisely, that showing provocative content makes people want to share...

Why sex doesn't sell

Sharing is what makes something go viral. The more people feel compelled to share something with others in their network, the more viral something will become.

This concept of sharing is not new. Marketers have known for a long time that word-of-mouth is a powerful force contributing to the success of a brand. Back in the day people would hear from their friends, family or work colleagues about things that caught everyone's interest. Perhaps there was an interesting billboard on the drive into work, or maybe an extra creative advertisement on TV the night before. People might mention it while chatting around the watercooler, or at a party. Nowadays of course, most people are connected to each other online. The internet has evolved into a tool that creates and manages social connections and community. If someone has some information that they think has some value, they'll share it with others through digital networks. News travels fast online, and something that has value can go viral extremely quickly if people have a reason to share it.

Something might be very interesting to people online, but it won't go viral if there's no reason to share it. All content online that has a high number of views also has a high number of shares. There's a strong positive correlation between views and shares. If there's no reason to tell others about something, it won't go viral.

The reason why Cheryl's advertisement hadn't gone viral was because it had a disincentive to share. Most people would feel quite awkward sharing something sexually explicit in their social networks, since people don't necessarily know all their connections that well. People care about social norms, and people choose their actions based on what society expects. Most people care about signalling something weird about their personality to others. People share things online not just because it's interesting, but also because they care about what other people think. When it comes to online advertising, sex doesn't sell because it's not very shareable.

Social currency

Any interpersonal value that people earn from interacting and being social with others. Social currency ensures you have a good reputation, people respect you and that you feel a sense of belonging.

When social status causes viral sharing

I used to work with a woman many years ago who would bring homemade cakes to work for everyone to eat. I was grateful to her when eating her cake, and she was a lovely person, but I often wondered what her motives for doing this were. Was she just being nice? Or was there some other reason? If she'd brought a different flavoured cake each time I might have assumed she did it out of her love of baking. But she only ever brought banana cake or raspberry sponge.

Psychologists might argue that her motives for bringing cakes to work were driven by a desire to earn 'social currency'. Social currency is a kind of value that people earn from interacting and being social with others. When you have social currency you have a good reputation, people respect you, and you feel a sense of belonging. Generally, the more social currency you have, the better your social status. It is likely that at some point in her life she learned that when she brought things to a group that everyone appreciated, people liked her more.

One way people earn social currency is by contributing in a positive way to a group. Ever wonder why some men watch sports that they don't actually play? Oftentimes it's so they can use their knowledge of the sport to manage their membership when socialising with other men. Shared interests are one of the forces that bind a group together. We learn from a young age that when we make people laugh they like us more and treat us better. When we're kind to others, they're usually kind in return. When we co-operate in a team, the team values our membership and we earn respect.

So why is social currency so important to people?

According to biologists, people's desire to earn social currency has evolved from an evolutionary process to ensure survival. Back in the early years of human existence, it was advantageous for people to be in groups because it gave everyone a better chance of success when hunting for food, and a better chance of surviving against predator attacks. Over time, to ensure the group stayed together and functioned properly, status and social hierarchies evolved. This meant that people had to learn group customs and communication styles to ensure in-group conflict was kept to a minimum. Group harmony was and still is necessary for groups to function well. The way to move up in a group's social hierarchy is to 'earn' it. In other words, earn social currency.

Social currency acts as a powerful motivator for people to share information with others. Understanding how people use information to build social currency is critical to understanding how something goes viral. People will share a humorous image, a joke, an idea, a movie, or any other information if they feel that other people will appreciate their efforts to share something that has value. People appreciate others who share useful information, which results in the sharer earning social currency.

It's not about controversy

One of the oldest mantras in marketing is that 'sex sells'. Instances of scantily clad women can be found in advertising as far back as 1871 when Pearl Tobacco used an illustration of a naked woman on their tobacco package. Calvin Klein were quite successful using sex appeal advertising in the 1980s, featuring near-naked male bodies on billboards, and the infamous model Brooke Shields exclaiming: 'You wanna know what comes between me and my Calvins? Nothing.' The aim of sex appeal advertising was to not only associate the brand with desirability, but to also create controversy.

The theory behind controversy is that if you do something that's taboo, then people will start talking about it. The brand might take a bit of a hit, since usually the controversy is something that's not really socially appropriate for a lot of people, but at least the brand gets some talk time. In this day and age, controversy doesn't fit the way things work anymore.

In 2011 Benetton released their 'Unhate' advertising campaign that featured cleverly photoshopped images of world leaders passionately kissing each other. One of the images featured the Pope kissing a senior Islamic leader. The image was awkward and difficult to look at without grimacing, even for people who aren't very religious. The Vatican got so outraged they threatened legal action unless the images were removed.

Although the campaign featured in the world's most well-known tabloids, it never went viral. It was not on social media, and no one was sharing it. In fact, the only place you could really find the images was on news websites reporting on the Vatican's response. There was no motive to share any of the images in the campaign. The topic of religion as a conversation piece is pretty much taboo in most cultures, further adding to the stigmatism of sharing.

The Benetton example illustrates how controversy isn't the best strategy for going viral. No one wants other people forming opinions about them that might tarnish their public image. In the digital economy, marketers need to think about creating content that's shareable. The way to do that is by pushing out content that has share value. If something can earn someone social capital, they'll share it.

The most shared image of all time

Shortly after winning the 2012 election, Barack Obama posted an image of himself hugging his wife Michelle on Facebook, with the caption 'Four more years'. Just 15 hours later the image had over 3.5 million Facebook 'Likes' and nearly half a million 'Shares'. To date it's the most shared image on Facebook ever.

Figure 1.1   Source: © ZUMA Press, Inc./Alamy Stock Photo

Barack Obama is obviously a popular man since so many people voted for him. But how did an image of him hugging his wife go viral?

When you look at the expression on Barack Obama's face in the photo, one thing that's clear is that the hug was obviously genuine and not staged. It's the same expression you see when somebody hasn't seen a loved one in a long while, and they finally meet and hug each other – kind of a mix of serenity and joy. In a rare moment people saw a very humanistic side to one of the most powerful men in the world.

Think about the leaders you've come across in your lifetime. What distinguished the leaders you respected from the leaders you despised? Was it their ability to be fair, to genuinely care about those who were being led, showing almost nurturing type qualities while caring for everyone's well-being? These are the basic qualities of the most respected leaders in history, though we rarely get to see genuine evidence of these qualities in our politicians. We might see news footage of them visiting schools or poor communities, but it's often difficult to separate their actions from their agenda, especially when it's close to elections. Watching this humanistic side of their new president made people feel safe that they had elected someone who had feelings. This was the man who would be running their country in times of difficulty over the next four years, and for those who voted for him this photo summed up good news that people felt compelled to share.

The image of Barack Obama hugging his wife is also shareable because it's based on a current event that many people are already talking about. When someone's already thinking about an event that's just happened, or something that's in the news, they're more likely to take notice of your content if it's also about that event. Riding the wave of a topic that's already being talked about by everybody is a useful shortcut to take.

An app gone viral

In 2013, two frat brothers at Furman University, South Carolina, got together to brainstorm an idea for a mobile phone app. Tyler Droll and Stephen 'Brooks' Buffington had built phone apps before, but none of their previous attempts had really taken off the way they would have liked.

They knew they could do better, and with true entrepreneurial spirit decided to keep plugging away at it until they produced a winner.

They met in a café and began bouncing new ideas off each other. One idea that stuck was a chat app where students at their university could post comments about anything they liked. No photos, and no video, just text-based chat. But with a difference – all chats would be completely anonymous.

Tyler got to work, and within a week had a working prototype. To get people using the app, Tyler and Brooks told their friends they'd made the app at the request of some Ivy Leaguers at Harvard. They were trying to associate it with Facebook's success in the movie *The Social Network* (2010). Their white lie paid off as their friends soon became hooked on the allure of anonymous chat, and within a week half of the university were using the app. After a few more weeks the app's popularity spread to a university down the road, then to another university across town. After just a few months the app had over 100,000 users as it rapidly took over university campuses across America. Within a year, the app had over two million users, and was in the top three most downloaded apps on Apple's App Store. The app had gone viral.

One unique feature about Yik Yak is that it has an upvote and downvote option. Yik Yak's unique ability to allow users to up or down vote serves two functions. First, when a post receives more than four downvotes the comment gets automatically removed. This creates a self-moderating system by empowering all users to remove undesirable comments, while at the same time gives users a direct measure of the value of their post. It's a direct measure of social currency – if people upvote it gives the user some credibility.

The other unique feature of Yik Yak is that it's anonymous. There's no registration or log in – people can post whatever they want completely anonymously. In general, people fear judgement from others on their actions and what they say, which restricts people's desire to speak freely. It takes a great deal of courage for somebody to speak out on something that goes against social norms. Even if it's right, and everyone else is wrong, people fear repercussions. History is full of people who stood up to express their opinion and got punished for it. Most people prefer to follow social norms, even when their true beliefs differ from the majority.

The anonymous feature in Yik Yak removes social bias that hinders people's ability to earn social currency, by creating a level playing field. Under normal circumstances people's ability to earn social currency is affected by social status. I'm sure you've noticed at your workplace or elsewhere that people who are liked get more laughs and pats on the back when they crack a joke, than someone who is less liked, even if they crack the same joke. The popular person earns more social currency than the less popular person, since people's perceptions of the less popular person bias their evaluation of reward and entitlement. Yik Yak removes this 'unfair advantage' by making everyone anonymous.

The anonymity of Yik Yak empowers people to speak freely without the bias of social status, and the social norms affecting freedom of expression. Yik Yak provides a sort of safe testing ground for people to test their true beliefs, and get rewarded for what they truly think. The feeling of getting 20 upvotes on something you've written is a powerful motivator to use the app, and makes it easy to get a shot of self-esteem. Yik Yak takes advantage of people's desire to earn social currency, by removing the social bias that inhibits people from sharing.

The secret to creating viral content is giving people a reason to share. Interesting content in itself isn't enough for content to go viral. The more shareable content is, and provided the content is shareable for a large number of people, the more likely it is that the content will go viral. If the content isn't shareable, or enough people aren't motivated to share, the content won't go viral. In this day of social connectedness the starting point is no longer how to create interest – it's how to motivate share.

Action plan for viral sharing

The secret to creating something that goes viral is to create a reason to share. There are three guiding principles or laws that should be adhered to from the ideation stage at campaign conception, through to final production and release:

1   Every decision guiding the development of an online campaign should be based on motivating consumers' reasons to share.

2   Every care in the development of an online campaign should be taken to eliminate or minimise consumers' reasons to not share.

3   The main motive to share your content must be chosen from a careful evaluation of (a) the strength of the motive to share, and (b) the number of people who have the motive to share.

Let me expand on these three principles.

The first step during the idea generation phase is to think about a possible reason why many people have to share information with others in their network. The obvious choice is humour, since everyone likes a good laugh, and everyone likes to share funny things. Although humour is the obvious choice, it does have some drawbacks. People have different styles of humour, and not everyone likes the same jokes, so the effectiveness of choosing humour is not guaranteed. Generally, the humour found in viral content tends to be laugh-out-loud funny, rather than simply amusing. The internet is littered with humorous marketing campaigns that failed to appeal to a wide enough audience.

Alternatives to humour as a motive to share are as follows:

Sharing a want. People have a tendency and desire to tell others about their wants and wishes. It's a mainstay of conversation: 'One day I want to visit... ' or 'I saw an amazing pair of shoes that I want...' If you give someone a picture of a particular pair of shoes that they want to own, they'll show it to people they know. The social website Pinterest is a great example of this.

The problem is that people's wants and wishes are not always universal – the person who is shown the picture of the shoes won't in turn share it with someone else if they don't also have a strong desire to own the same shoes. Therefore, the trick is to identify a want or wish that everyone wants at the same point in time. Consider, for example, the pain people feel stuck in a dull work routine during the middle of winter, with no holiday in sight. It's safe to say there would be significant numbers of people in this predicament. It's also safe to say that most if not all of the people in this predicament have a strong desire to escape. Therefore, something like an image of an ocean villa in tropical Bora Bora would likely appeal to these people in the sense of wanting to escape to paradise quite urgently. People would feel an urge to share the picture, particularly if they know others in their network are in the same predicament. There have been several idyllic location-based photos that have gone viral in this way.

Other options could include products that solve a well-defined problem that's suffered by many, situations that almost everyone would rather avoid, or unusual situations that most people would like to experience.

Making people look interesting. People want to be perceived as interesting, since interesting people are liked, and it earns them social currency. One way people portray themselves as interesting is by saying interesting or witty things, but not everyone has a natural ability to entertain in this way. Inspirational type content makes the person who is sharing appear interesting, since the ability to inspire is associated with strength of character and diversity of knowledge. A pre-packaged image with an inspiring quote is one example, though any content that provokes thoughtful reflection can make the sharer look interesting.

Signalling to others something about their value system. Everyone has a value system: a set of beliefs they care about passionately. People are motivated to let others know about their beliefs, but sharing these beliefs in a way that makes people take notice, and without sounding trite, can be difficult.

Consider the example of someone who believes that active duty soldiers are insufficiently recognised for their services to the nation. Perhaps they know someone who is in the services, or it could be that they are patriotic. Stating their beliefs directly might be acknowledged by others, but it's unlikely to be shared, despite the importance. People are wary of sounding too 'intense', especially with people they might not know that well. But sharing an image of a soldier clutching his newborn baby and weeping, just before he returns for another tour of active duty, is an indirect moderate way to share their belief with others, since the image was not produced by the sender, only passed on. Packaged in this way the image packs a powerful message, but is shareable.

Sharing a want, making people look interesting, and providing a way for people to share their core values indirectly without being too intense are three motives to share that can provide the starting point for an online campaign.

It's important through the development process to also ensure reasons to not share are avoided. One way to monitor and evaluate disincentives to share is by evaluating likely emotions that the viewer will experience. Generally, though with some exceptions, negative emotions should be avoided since most people don't have a tendency or desire to make others feel bad (by sharing something that evokes negative emotions). Content of a sexual nature might capture people's attention, but it can also create feelings of awkwardness, and therefore severely inhibits sharing. Content that shocks can cause disgust, and content highlighting people's misfortunes can cause sadness. Although powerful, you should use emotions such as these with caution.

One category that's the exception to this rule is content that's centred on empathy and deservingness. An image of a father who changed his looks to match his child's deformity, and an image of a woman who slept next to her husband's coffin one last time before he was buried, both went viral and created powerful emotions. They were shareable because they exposed a side of humanity that revealed frailty. Since we're all exposed to the same conditions in life, many beyond our control, people will empathise and share content that suggests an unfair disadvantage, or dutiful effort in the face of adversity (for more on this subject please refer to **Chapter 6**).

2

Self-enhancement

In 1974, a young professor in Hungary wanted to solve a problem in design engineering. He taught architecture, and no one had yet figured out how to hold objects together where each object could be moved independently, without the sum of all the objects falling apart. Arguably its practical usefulness would be limited, but driven by his academic curiosity he thought the design would at least be useful for teaching his architectural students about the form and space of three-dimensional objects.

His first attempt at solving the problem was to hand-carve several cubes, and join them together using rubber bands. This failed. He then considered how he could hold together a collection of independently moving objects, by using the shape of the object itself. After much trial and error he drafted some blueprints, comprising 26 small cubes all held together using only their shape, where each cube could occupy any position in the arrangement without removing the cube from the entire object. He carved a prototype from his blueprints in wood, and pasted coloured stickers on each cube face so he could track the movement of each cube. After playing around with his prototype, he was delighted to find that this cube structure worked. The only problem was, when each cube was out of its original position it was extremely difficult to get it back into the original position since all cubes got jumbled very quickly. 'We turn the cube and it twists us,' he thought to himself.

Although he didn't realise it at the time, Ernő Rubik, the young professor from Hungary, had just invented the biggest selling toy in history.

How a frustrating puzzle became the biggest selling toy in history

Over 350 million Rubik's Cubes have been sold worldwide. It's estimated that one out of every seven people alive have tried to solve one. What makes it so popular?

A Rubik's Cube has over 42 quintillion combinations, and just one solution. But intriguingly, according to mathematical calculations, every Rubik's Cube can be solved in fewer than 20 twists. This creates an unusual challenge. It's not uncommon to hear of people who can solve the puzzle in under a minute. 'Cubic Rubes' as they're called are Rubik's Cube fans who are members of Cube Clubs. Many of them regularly solve the puzzle in less than ten seconds. At the time of writing Collin Burns from the USA holds the world record for solving the puzzle in just 5.25 seconds. (How is that even possible! For anyone who has tried to solve it and failed, like me, the notion that someone else can solve the puzzle in seconds seems quite bizarre.)

When the Rubik's Cube hit the shelves for the first time in the 1980s, on the box it was advertised: 'Over a billion positions, but just one solution'. The cube looked deceptively simple to solve, sitting there in its see-through plastic wrapping, and the claim of a billion positions combined with its unique appearance invited people to accept the challenge. News soon spread of some people being able to solve the puzzle in seconds. It was the perfect ultimate challenge – something that's impossible, yet something that everyone should be capable of doing. There are few things in this world that have replicated a challenge this unique.

When the Rubik's Cube first came out, people everywhere were compelled to try to join the special club of people who could solve it. Those who knew how to solve it were held in awe and admired for their ability to solve the impossible. The secret to the cube's success was that it created the ultimate mental challenge: solve something that's impossible but that some people can solve in seconds. This is what's so unique about the Rubik's Cube. Many toys offer the player a challenge, but few of them do it on this scale.

Our natural tendency to criticise others

I often see puzzles on social media networks that have gone viral. 'This puzzle was taken from a Kindergarten entrance exam in Hong Kong. Can you solve it?' Or '92% of Americans got this wrong. Can you get it?' These puzzles almost always suggest that 'less clever people than you can solve it, what about you?' Like the Rubik's Cube claiming to have a billion positions, yet everyday some people solve it in seconds. The invitation for people to have a go is strong. People feel compelled to share these challenges with others.

Self-enhancement

A psychological tendency people have to feel good about themselves, and maintain their self-esteem.

Humans are oddly attracted to challenges, and many puzzles are simply invitations to be challenged. Challenges are attractive to people because of 'self-enhancement', which is a psychological tendency we all have to feel good about ourselves. It manifests itself as things we do to boost our self-esteem. To self-enhance, we'll tend to accentuate the positive things about ourselves, and downplay the negative things. For example, we're more likely to emphasise our positive traits, and point out other people's negative traits, because that makes us feel better. We're more likely to tell other people about the time someone else at work embarrassed themselves, than when we embarrassed ourselves. We tend to talk about our achievements, and talk about other people's failures. Although most people don't consciously realise it, positioning other people as lower than ourselves has a self-enhancing effect, by making us feel better.

I had a friend once who used to love watching reality shows about people on death row, and the violence of the American prison system. I asked him one day why he enjoyed watching that kind of stuff, and he told me that the problems the men had in prison made his own problems seem more trivial, which cheered him up. Rather than make him feel depressed, watching the suffering of others nurtured his self-esteem. This is essentially how self-enhancement works. Positioning ourselves against the misfortunes of others is another way people self-enhance.

As part of self-enhancement, we all have a tendency to have overly positive evaluations of ourselves, think we have more control over our destiny than we actually do, and for the most part be overly optimistic. Gamblers for example may think they're good at gambling, have a better chance of winning than the statistics would suggest. Accordingly, gamblers often convince themselves that this time they won't fail. Self-enhancement motives convince the gambler that they can win.

When I was younger I used to work in the ski industry as a ski patroller. Part of my job was to put up fences to protect skiers and boarders from dangerous rock outcrops or other hazards, particularly beginners who were prone to injury from losing control. One thing that helped me plan the courses was knowing that beginner skiers and boarders tended to ski as far away from the lift as possible, and advanced skiers and boarders tended to ski as close to the lift as possible. Those who were advanced had invested considerable time becoming as good as they were, and their way to self-enhance was to show off their skills to other people who were riding the lift up. Those who were beginners didn't want other people to watch them falling down. In my years in the ski industry I learned that the most popular lifts for advanced skiers had their advanced runs in sight of the chairlifts. The desire to self-enhance is tied to our desire to want to be better than others.

If you ask people if they would rather be on the winning team or the losing team, they'll choose winning team every time. If you were one of the special few who could solve the Rubik's Cube, you were better than people who couldn't. Everybody wants to be admired, and the desire to be admired influences our tendency to self-enhance. The Rubik's Cube seems an impossible puzzle, yet we all know or have heard of people who have conquered it. These people earn admiration from others and are regarded as having some special skills that we don't possess. Because we don't like being lower in status than others, we want to be like those who are better than ourselves.

Are your friends trying to make you jealous?

Someone once told me that the only reason people post status updates on Facebook is to make other people jealous. Well this might not be true exactly – no one wants to be known as an egotist. But it is true that people will share content for a reason. Oftentimes people share content to maintain their self-esteem and personal worth. In other words, people share content online to self-enhance.

You can easily find evidence of people sharing bloated information to self-enhance on dating websites. There, people tend to portray themselves as who they want to be rather than who they actually are. An interesting study done recently in the USA and the UK found that the number one exaggeration for men on dating websites was having a better job than they actually had, and the number one exaggeration for women was their weight being lower than it actually was (*Opinion Matters*, 2011).

So it's not necessarily that your friends are trying to make you jealous, but rather that they're attempting to put themselves in a good light in comparison to others. That photo of your friend on an exotic trekking holiday is designed to make them feel good, not make you feel bad, even though it might have the unintended effect of making you feel envious. Knowing that others in their network might not have the same opportunity as them improves their self-esteem.

One way to get a shot of self-esteem is from positive feedback. On social media this usually means earning a 'Like', positive 'Comment', or 'Share' (or variations thereof depending on the brand of social media network being used). These are called 'approval cues'. People get a shot of self-esteem when someone appraises something they've shared.

Approval cues

A tendency for people to seek approval from others from information shared.

Getting positive recognition for sharing something on social media is like a pat on the back, or a thankyou. It helps the sharer to feel good about themselves.

Younger people tend to use approval cues more than older age groups. Observation studies of teenagers using social media have discovered one peculiar behaviour in particular that sets them apart – teenagers will post or share something on Facebook, but then they'll monitor the post to gauge the volume of reactions. After a set amount of time, if the number of resulting 'Likes' and 'Shares' is too low, they'll delete the content. Sometimes within the first ten minutes! Their aim of posting is to earn recognition for what they're sharing as a way to self-enhance. If the recognition is insufficient, they'd rather delete the content than suffer perceived judgement from others against their failed efforts to self-enhance. Not getting a reaction has a *negative* effect on their self-esteem.

Why goths wear black

In a disturbing study conducted on the gothic subculture, researchers found higher than normal incidences of self-harm and suicide among goths (Young *et al.*, 2006). But the reason for the higher incidences of self-harm and suicide wasn't related to the gothic subculture itself, but rather that people who already had these inclinations were more likely to join the gothic subculture, because their perception was that gothics were into that kind of thing. Of course it becomes a self-fulfilling prophecy – the more people who have a tendency to self-harm or commit suicide that join the gothic subculture, the more people who have the same tendencies will join in the future.

Figure 2.1 Source: © Catchlight Visual Services/Alamy Stock Photo

Part of being a goth is looking the part, with the black clothes, black nail polish, and pale skin. Goths want to look morbid. As with other groups in society, members of the gothic subculture are bound by the same values, beliefs and interests.

Membership cues

A tendency for people to share information with others to legitimise their group membership.

Hipsters grow big beards, sports fans wear their team colours, and surfers wear board shorts. Why? It's because humans are tribal. Wearing the outfits and adornments of a group in society signals to others which group we identify with. Most often our choice of group is decided from the ideals and values of the group. If we're a morbid person who thinks life isn't worth living after 30, and that wearing clothes that go against society's expectations is a good thing, then likely we'll find the gothic culture quite attractive.

People's desire to express who they are, and signal to others something unique about their choice of group membership, is called 'membership cues'. Goths will adorn their black regalia to signal to other people their membership to the gothic subculture.

Membership cues are important because they give marketers insight into what types of content their target audience is likely to share. Gothic conversation is likely to revolve around gothic music, gothic-looking clothes or something else they all share an interest in. Goths use membership cues in conversations to validate their shared membership. Sharing images of a gothic nature allows members of the goth subculture to signal their allegiance and membership, just like wearing black.

Board shorts and the environment

Surfing is part of the culture in Australia, and one thing that all surfers value is the search for the perfect wave. Australian surf brand Quiksilver wanted to appeal to their target market by integrating the freedom and lifestyle of the surf culture with a unique location. Rather than the usual beach scene, they set the scene in the middle of a city.

The video ad (**https://youtu.be/JR_naKxLEPc**) begins by showing a group of young men walking the streets, with one of them holding a surfboard under their arm. The movie uses shaky low-resolution footage to create the illusion that the group are being filmed happenstance by someone with a mobile phone. They come across a city pond with a bridge over it. The one with the surfboard unzips it from its cover, and paddles out into the middle of the pond. As he's paddling out the rest of the men start crossing the bridge. When they're halfway across, they produce a cluster of dynamite sticks. One of them lights the dynamite and lobs it into the pond. The resulting explosion causes a huge wake that turns into a six foot wave. The man with the surfboard paddles to catch the wave, and starts surfing it. Punk music plays as his friends whoop and holler in the background.

The movie struck a chord with the surfing community and spread very quickly. Not only was the video ad very cool, it also sparked debate over its authenticity. Of course the video was fake, but that didn't stop people wondering if it was possible to produce a wave from an explosion that could be surfed.

Part of the reason why the Quiksilver video got shared was because it provided an interesting topic of conversation. But there's another important reason why it got shared and eventually went viral. The movie enabled people who were into surfing to self-enhance. People shared the movie to signal to other surfers something about their values and ideals, and validate their membership status as a fellow surfer. The movie was a membership cue that surfers used to validate their allegiance.

In my younger days I spent time living in Europe, working in Austrian ski resorts in the winters and bartending in the summers. One of the cities I spent some time in was Munich. Germany doesn't have much coastline, and Munich is about as far as it gets in Europe from the ocean. But the city did have a small community of passionate surfers, and the most unique surf spot in Europe – 'The Eisbach'. It's a unique river wave that's formed from river water flowing through a tunnel in the middle of the city. The wave isn't as big as waves in the ocean, it gets pretty cold, and there's no sandy beach. But surfers from all over the world converge on this spot because it's the only urban wave of its kind in the world.

The popularity of The Eisbach in Munich illustrates something important about the surfer culture – there's more to the culture of surfing than just surfing big waves. Surfers spend a lot of time talking about surfing locations – the more unique the location you've surfed, the more credence and respect you have. It's like earning a badge of honour. The surfing lifestyle is not just about surfing, it's also about freedom. Surfers are not only bound together by their love of surfing, they're also bound together by their love of the surfing culture that goes with it.

The Quiksilver video was similarly set under unique conditions. Groups are bound by shared values and ideals, and people use information that's consistent with those values and ideals as a way to remind others of their legitimate membership. By sharing the Quiksilver video, it enabled surfers to signal to each other something about their ideals and values that legitimised their claim of being a true surfer.

Another image that was heavily shared among the surfing community in 2013 was one in which a surfer was riding inside the barrel of a large wave. The photo was taken at Java, an iconic surf location in Indonesia. It's a very common scene used for surf advertisements, but this one had a special difference. The difference was that there were pieces of pollution clearly visible in the water, including food wrappers and other organic material that obviously didn't belong. The image of the man surfing a beautifully perfect wave with clear blue skies, though tainted by the presence of so much pollution created a sharp contrast. If you're a member of the surfing culture you'll know that the health of the ocean is something that all surfers hold dear to their hearts. The image was highly shareable because it enabled surfers to signal membership cues based on their environmental concerns at a legendary surf spot. The only difference between the Quiksilver pollution ad and any other typical surf ad was the presence of the pollution. The typical image of a man surfing a perfect wave would likely never have gone viral, because it's something that's tied to surfers' interests rather than their core value system. Things that get shared tend to appeal to people's value systems more than just appealing to their interests.

People self-enhance in different ways

People share content as a way to self-enhance. A motorcycle enthusiast might share images of interesting motorcycles, a surfer might share videos of surfing, and an environmentalist might share images of pollution. The goal of sharing is for a person to signal something about themselves to others. All sharing based on self-enhancement motives aims to achieve this goal. But what differs between people is *why* they want to signal something about themselves. The middle-aged motorcycle enthusiast might share images of motorcycles with friends to send an implicit message that he's still young at heart, in defiance against growing old. The surfer might share surfing movies to remind his colleagues of his own skill and experience at surfing. The environmentalist might share images of pollution to help rally support for an upcoming protest. People share not only to signal something about themselves, but also to shape other people's impressions. This is called 'impression management'.

Whenever I see a picture on Facebook that's getting thousands of shares, I always pause to see if I can figure out why. Oftentimes it's fairly easy to unravel – the image is exceptionally funny (emotion), or resonates with people because it places a current event in an interesting light (affinity). But one picture I came across had me puzzled. The picture is cartoon like, but not cute. It's split into two, with a variation of the same image on the top and the bottom. In the top image three men are pulling a rope connected to a

Impression management

A tendency for people to share information with others to signal something about a meaningful character trait.

large heavy block, much like you would expect to see in ancient Egypt with workers hauling giant stones to the pyramids. On top of the block is a man sitting at a desk, directing the workers to pull harder. On the block is written 'business' and on the desk is written 'boss'.

The picture underneath is the same, except there is no desk or boss sitting on top of the big block being pulled. Instead, there's an extra man who is in front of the other workers also pulling the rope. An arrow points to that man and says 'leader'.

The message in the meme is that being a boss does not necessarily mean you're a leader, and that leadership is demonstrated by leading workers the way forward, not directing them. Obviously this is an admirable viewpoint to have for anyone with ambition in the workforce. The obvious reason for sharing such an image would be to signal to others something about your business acumen, or your suitability for leadership. But this didn't really explain why it had gone viral, since it isn't the type of thing people would share with their friends on Facebook. I remained puzzled for a while, until I learned something of interest about people in their late teens to early 20s that made it all make sense.

Digital natives

People born in the early 1990s who have always known the internet.

'Digital natives' are those younger folk who've grown up with the internet – people born in the 1990s. Within this group are those who were brought up with the social side of the internet (Web 2.0) – people in their late teens to early 20s. They would have been about five years old when Myspace was the social platform of choice, and ten years old when Facebook started to become popular. I call these people 'social natives'. For this demographic, using social tools on digital technologies is nothing new – for them being social with others through digital networks had always been there.

Social natives

People born in the early 1990s who were brought up with social media on the internet.

Unlike many of the older generation who remember a time before the internet, social natives view public-facing social media platforms like Facebook and Twitter in a slightly different way. They're very conscious of the fact that mainstream social media platforms are public places, kind of like the city square. It's neutral ground where they connect with not only friends, but also colleagues and family members. Like the city square, this is not the place for shenanigans.

Facebook is where you dress up and put your best foot forward. If you want to let your hair down and play up a bit, you go somewhere private. Social natives keep the wild party selfies and other shenanigans on private networks, like Snapchat or Line. What I discovered after doing some research on this demographic is that a significant proportion of digital natives use Facebook to create and maintain a clean positive image of themselves. They understand that people research other people online, including Facebook, to get a glimpse of the real person behind the resume. This includes prospective employers. Social natives don't bother with privacy settings, Facebook is a tool to show the world what a great person you are. As it turns out, the people who were sharing the 'boss' image were all in their final year at university. It was a classic case of self-enhanced 'impression management'.

People are biologically programmed to feel good about themselves and nurture their wellbeing through self-enhancement. Given the importance of self-enhancement motives, we often see evidence of it in viral content. For marketers this provides a tremendous opportunity by providing a clear path for branded marketing content sharing.

Creating shareable content around self-enhancement motives needn't be a difficult puzzle to solve if you have an understanding of your target audience, their values, beliefs, and what they care about. Often self-enhancement motives are based on group membership, which is the best place to start. Once you get insight into the values and beliefs of your target audience, it's simply a matter of appealing to those values and beliefs, by giving them a reason to share using membership cues, impression management, or approval cues.

Action plan for self-enhancement

People self-enhance in different ways, and for different reasons. Understanding self-enhancement motives in your target audience is a critical step in the initial phases of creating an online marketing campaign. This requires an understanding of not just their demographic characteristics, but also their psychographic preferences – their values and ideals. It's often not so obvious what people care about. If you're not part of the group culture yourself, you have to do some digging.

One way to gain insight into your target audience's values and ideals is to listen in and observe their behaviour. Find out where they hang out. This doesn't necessarily mean you need to stalk them in the real world. It could be as simple as joining the same Facebook groups or discussion groups. Of course you could also run focus groups if you have a budget. The aim is to figure out what really matters to them, what ideals they would stand up for, and what it is about the world that they would miss the most if it were gone.

As my discussion earlier about the surfing culture illustrates, oftentimes it's not the obvious that matters, but rather the culture of the group they belong to that they really care about. Surfers are not inclined to share just any picture or video of someone surfing a wave – they all surf, and there's nothing so special about sharing an image of someone else surfing. While researching a target audience you have to dig deeper to discover what it is about their value system that binds them together.

The starting point for crafting shareable content based on self-enhancement motives is to identify shared core values in your target audience. Once you know what matters to your target audience, the next step when creating self-enhancement motives to share is to design a reason for sharing. As outlined in this chapter, there are three reasons for sharing to self-enhance:

1   **Membership cues.** Recall that members of a group are bound by common values or beliefs. If you attend the group's social meetings you'll eventually discover what those values and beliefs are – since the topics of conversation give clues about what they might be. Motorcycle clubs will mostly talk about the lifestyle of riding a motorcycle, such as near misses with cars, or long distance adventure tours. These are membership cues – basically things that members in the group think are important and that they all share an interest in. People use membership cues in conversation to confirm their membership in the group, like showing your ticket to get into the show. Shareable membership cue materials for motorcycle enthusiasts might include things like 'dash cam' footage of motorcycle vs. car conflicts, unique motorcycle tour moments, or motorcycle sports achievements. If your target audience are motorcycle enthusiasts, any of these would aid motorcycle enthusiasts to signal their membership legitimacy.

2   **Impression management.** People share content to manage other people's impressions of themselves. The usefulness of content that can shape people's opinions is that it circumvents the need to inflate their ego or say something directly that other people might find cocky. Content that enables people to manage impressions includes anything that signals something about a character trait that is revered. For example, a middle-aged man might share a picture of a customised motorcycle to remind his peers about his passion for freedom, rebelliousness against the ageing process, and connection to his youth. Note that his reason for sharing might not necessarily be to seek agreement from his network over the beauty of the machine.

3   **Approval cues.** There's nothing like the feeling of approval from those around you. When you get applause, or a laugh, or even a simple pat on the back, it can give you a tremendous boost in self-esteem. The equivalent of this in social media is the 'Like', 'Retweet', or 'Thumbs up' (depending on the social media platform). When people share something under this motive, they're seeking approval from others. Some types of things people share to earn approval cues include: recent purchases made, recent sporting or life achievements, or amusing situations.

3

Emotion

When I first met my brother-in-law, Trevor, he was a London taxi driver. Born and bred in East London, we quite often met after work in his old neighbourhood to play darts. I loved going to the pub with Trevor because he always had the most interesting stories to tell, particularly entertaining in his cockney accent. Like the time he picked up the lead singer from one of the world's biggest rock bands. So Trevor told it, the singer was blind drunk, and couldn't remember where he was staying. After finally arriving at his hotel, Trevor made him sing one of his famous songs to pay for his fare.

Trevor had an interesting life, but the time eventually came when he parked his 'sherbet dab' (cab) for the last time to look for greener pastures.

Trevor's personality made it easy for him to make new friends, and he discovered he had a knack for selling. After several years of job hopping between sales jobs he found himself an executive position in a large education company. The job was well paid, and mostly involved travelling around the world to meet with prospective clients. It was a dream job – he earned frequent flight upgrades and stayed in luxurious hotels in exotic locations. That is until one day when it all changed.

Trevor was asked to go to Christchurch in New Zealand to meet with some clients. But something terrible happened. As he was rushing through a crowded market to meet his clients, the Christchurch earthquake struck. In the wrong place at the wrong time, Trevor made a narrow escape, just missing a building collapse as he ran for safety. It was one of New Zealand's biggest natural disasters that tragically claimed 185 lives. Trevor had a near-death experience.

Trevor's flower shop

If you've ever met anyone who's had a near-death experience, you'll know that it has a dramatic effect on their outlook on life. They often make big changes, and Trevor was no different. He developed an irresistible urge to take control over his life, and spend more time with people who mattered to him. Trevor told me he suddenly realised that his family was more important to him than anything else, and that he wanted to spend more time with them. To everyone's surprise, Trevor quit his dream job and bought a flower shop in a small town by the sea.

Soon after Trevor took ownership, he found himself alone in his shop with his head in his hands. The reality of his decisions was weighing heavy. He didn't know the names of most of the flowers, or how to arrange them into bouquets. Worse, he began to doubt whether he had the skills or knowledge to run a business. After two weeks of searching the internet struggling to teach himself the art of floristry, he decided the wisest thing would be to hire someone who knew what they were doing. He asked around his village and eventually found a young local woman who had some experience and training in floristry. She was cheerful and friendly with the customers, and was capable of producing beautiful bouquets. She gave Trevor some hope.

Soon after hiring the young woman, Trevor realised that he had another problem. One that was more difficult to fix. It seemed that having beautiful flower arrangements was not enough, because everyone in town was buying their flowers from a local superstore. Trevor was struggling to pay his bills, and began to wonder if he had made a mistake quitting his former job with security and regular income. He desperately wanted to make his new business work, and knew he had to find a way to turn things around.

After he had tucked his daughter into bed one night, Trevor grabbed a beer and sat on his porch staring into the darkness. He began to think how he could get his flower shop to work. Several hours passed and as he was just about to go back inside he noticed a red pickup truck drive slowly down his street, and stop just outside his neighbour's house. A young man hopped out of the truck clutching a bouquet of flowers, and headed for his neighbour's front door. After pausing for what seemed like a good few minutes, the young man finally rang the doorbell. A light in the window went on, and his neighbour's daughter appeared behind the door. She stepped outside, and closed the door quietly behind her. The young man presented the girl with the flowers. She accepted them with a blush, and then gave him a kiss on the cheek. Hand in hand they walked slowly towards his truck. He held the door open for her, hopped in the other side, and drove off slowly into the night. Trevor thought back to his first date with his wife and began to smile.

Then, he had an epiphany.

Trevor suddenly realised something he thought must be quite important. He realised that there was more to buying flowers than the actual flowers. He figured that if people's decisions to purchase flowers could be driven by emotions, then these emotions could override feelings of getting a good price or better-looking flowers, like from his competitors. This must be true, he thought, because happiness comes from relationships, not objects, and flowers let people know that they are loved. He'd been thinking about flowers the wrong way – buying flowers is about giving not buying.

To test his theory, Trevor devised an ingenious little experiment. Mother's Day was fast approaching and he bought a sandwich board and placed it on the footpath outside his shop with one of two different messages on it. Alternating each message, on one day the sandwich board read 'It's Mother's Day. Flowers to suit all budgets!' The message was designed to make people think of saving money when buying flowers. It was price focussed. On every other day he changed the message to: 'It is not happy people who are thankful. It is thankful people who are happy. Give flowers this Mother's Day!' This message was designed to make people think about the emotions they would experience when they presented the flowers to their mothers. It was emotion focussed.

> ### Tip
> When people focus on the outcome of an event, emotions are more likely to control their decision. When the emotions are strong, people will share with others.

He continued to alternate each message for the month leading up to Mother's Day. Then, after Mother's Day came and went, he calculated how many flowers he'd sold when the message was price focussed, compared to how many flowers he'd sold when the message was emotion focussed. To his delight, his calculations told him he sold 30 per cent more flowers when the message was emotion focussed.

Trevor, a cockney taxi driver running a flower shop, had discovered something quite remarkable: people's decisions are based on perceived outcomes, not just the here and now, and these outcomes when laden with emotion can act as powerful motivators to change how people behave. When the message was emotion focussed, it primed people to think about their mothers, and the reactions they would get when their mother received the flowers – an emotion-laden outcome. When the message was price focussed, people were drawn to think about the here and now, and simply the cost of the flowers. When people focus on the outcome of an event, emotions are more likely to control their decision. When the emotions are strong, people will share with others.

Emotions and sharing

There are several theories on what range of emotions exist, but most are consistent with Plutchik's theory, which proposes that the main emotions people (and animals) can experience include: joy, trust, fear, surprise, sadness, disgust, anger and anticipation. These emotions, when mixed in various combinations, can create new emotions. Awe, for example, is thought to be a mix of fear and surprise. Each of these emotions also has varying degrees of intensity. Intense joy is ecstasy, and intense surprise is amazement.

It might not seem so obvious, but we actually spend a significant amount of time organising our behaviours around emotions we expect to feel as a result of our actions. Consider the frivolous example of deciding whether or not to order dessert at a restaurant. Fundamentally our decision to do so might be based on how hungry we feel, or the price of the dessert. But underlying these basic thought processes is an assessment of the emotions we anticipate we'll feel as a result of our decision. People not only consider how hungry they are now, but also how hungry and weak they'll be later on if they don't eat. If someone anticipates feeling guilty and sad after eating the dessert, this sways their decision to not order the dessert. To satisfy their hunger they may instead opt for something healthier. But if they anticipate pleasure with no guilt, this sways their decision to order the dessert.

Plutchik's theory

According to Professor Robert Plutchik, the main emotions people can experience include: joy, trust, fear, surprise, sadness, disgust, anger and anticipation. All other emotions people feel are a combination of these.

The interesting thing about emotional decisions is that people will guess what emotions they'll feel after the experience, and start feeling those emotions before the experience takes place. If someone thinks they'll feel guilty after eating a dessert, then they'll start feeling guilty before they actually eat it. Or if they think they'll experience pleasure, they'll start feeling pleasure just waiting for the dessert to arrive. This is interesting because sometimes people will misjudge the emotion they expect to feel, and will therefore feel the wrong emotion before the event has taken place. Children sometimes do this when they have to go to the doctor. Even though the treatment given at the doctor is likely to increase their wellbeing and make them feel better afterwards, they feel fear that the doctor will do something to make them miserable afterwards, and therefore suffer tremendous anxiety before their appointment. After they've gone to the doctor they wonder what all the fuss was about. The emotion they felt before going to the doctor was misjudged.

Emotions felt from making the same decisions in the past also influence people's behaviour. If someone resisted ordering dessert in the past, and felt proud of themselves for resisting, then the next time they're faced with the decision on whether or not to order dessert they'll likely be successful resisting because they want to feel proud again. Recalling past emotions based on similar experiences is a powerful influencer on human behaviour. Sometimes people may anticipate a variety of conflicting emotions. Someone might anticipate the joy and serenity of eating a particularly delicious looking dessert, but also feel anticipation waiting for the dessert, and self-loathing after eating the dessert. According to Plutchik's theory, people often experience more than one emotion when making a decision.

So how does this influence people's decisions to share content with others?

The secret to how emotion drives sharing is that people will not only tend to estimate the emotions they'll themselves feel after an experience, but they'll also try to estimate the emotions other people will feel. Before we share a joke we estimate whether the other person will like the joke, feel joy and laugh. If we expect the emotion from the other person will be positive, then we'll share it. If we think the emotion the other person will feel will be negative, or ambivalent, then likely we won't share it. When that person feels good because we shared something that made them feel good, that person feels grateful. When someone feels grateful it makes us feel good.

An estimation of how someone might react when sharing emotional content is a powerful driver of decisions to share.

Why a smile from a stranger makes us feel good

Have you ever walked into a room of people who are laughing and begun to feel more cheerful? Or had someone smile at you, and it made you feel good? Emotions are contagious – almost subconsciously our emotions can be affected by other people's emotions around us.

Emotions can transfer between people, and also transfer between groups of people. A whole community can get angry when just one resident in the street is too noisy, or a whole crowd can start to clap and cheer after a moving speech from a leader. So why does this contagion occur? Shared emotions spread because they facilitate mutual involvement, ease social interactions, and generally satisfy a deep rooted desire to belong when in a group. People want to be liked, and one way people try to be liked is by getting closer to other people. Emotion improves friendship, and in large groups it strengthens social bonds. One other reason people tend to follow and mimic group behaviour is because of a desire to remain anonymous – most people have a fear of being seen as different, so will adopt the mood and emotion of the group to fit in and not stand out.

It's important to understand how emotions transfer from video advertisements to the viewer, because the viewer must be affected by the emotions before they'll be motivated to share. Generally, the stronger the emotion felt by the viewer, the greater the likelihood that they'll share. But the problem is, how do you transfer the emotion from your video ad to the viewer? It's no good trying to create strong emotions in your video ad if those emotions don't transfer. For a video ad to be successful you have to affect the viewer in a strong way. The transfer of the emotion from the video ad to the viewer must be as efficient as possible.

Emotional contagion

An individual's tendency to feel the same emotions as other people around them.

One way to ensure the efficient transfer of emotions is to use something called 'emotional contagion'. Emotional contagion is where the emotional state of someone is affected by the emotional state of others. The best way to do that in a video ad is to transfer the emotions through facial expressions.

We wanted to understand how effective facial expressions were at transferring emotions from a movie to the viewer, and so we conducted an experiment. We randomly divided a group of students into two groups. We showed each of the groups the same short movie skit, which featured a group of people with sheets over their heads, like ghosts, creeping through a large public library that was busy with students studying. Obviously the prank attracted quite a bit of attention from the people in the library – it's not something anyone would expect to see. Some people began to smile, while others looked annoyed for interrupting their reading.

Figure 3.1   Source: © Veronica Louro/123rf.com

After around five minutes or so, three men dressed as 'Ghostbusters' entered the library, and began to chase the ghosts out with devices that kind of looked like vacuum cleaners. This created further commotion. Some of the library patrons looked amused, while some looked annoyed.

There were several cameras hidden around the library recording the prank. There was a mix of panoramic shots from a distance, and close-up shots of facial reactions. The facial expressions were of either annoyance or amusement.

Each group in our experiment was shown the exact same footage of the prank, but with one main difference. We removed the close-ups of people's facial expressions in one group. Our hypothesis was twofold. First that the emotions felt by the viewers who saw the close-ups of facial expressions would be stronger than the emotions felt by those viewers who did not see the facial expressions. Second, that those who saw the facial expressions would be more likely to share (since they would be more emotionally affected), than those who didn't see the facial expressions.

After analysing the data the results found that in the group where no close-ups of facial expressions were shown, 9 per cent shared the movie.

But in the group where facial expressions were shown, 64 per cent shared the movie. We confirmed our hypothesis that facial expressions helped the transfer of emotion, and that the strength of emotion boosted sharing.

A dramatic surprise on a quiet square

Superviral

An image, movie or idea that has over a million shares or five million views.

'A dramatic surprise on a quiet square' (**https://youtu.be/316AzLYfAzw**) is a video advertisement for the Belgium TV channel TNT. It's a 'superviral' with over four million shares. The movie features a large red button placed in the middle of a quiet city square, with a large sign over the button saying 'Push to add drama'. Passers-by stare at the button, but no one has the courage to push it. Finally a man on his bicycle stops, gathers courage, and pushes the button. Immediately a siren goes off, and a dramatic scene ensues.

The entire sequence involves a series of related stunts revolving around the evacuation of an injured man to hospital. The injured man falls out of the back of an ambulance, then a man on his bicycle crashes into the door of the ambulance that results in an ensuing fight with the ambulance officer. A black car of bad guys screeches to a halt and begins a gun fight, and a woman rides past on a motorcycle wearing lingerie. It is all staged in under two minutes.

The ad transfers several emotions, including surprise, happiness, disgust and fear, all by using the facial expressions of people in the square who are observing the drama. The ad illustrates how it's possible to transfer a wide variety of emotions. According to research by Paul Ekman, people can detect seven main emotions from facial expressions, including anger, disgust, sadness, fear, happiness, surprise and contempt (Ekman *et al.*, 1992). Interestingly, he found that people universally make the same face for each of these emotions, regardless of where they're from. He even found people who have been blind since birth make the same expressions.

The scenes of the movie dart back and forth between showing the ambulance drama as it unfolds, and the facial reactions of the people in the square who are observing the drama. What is important is the timing of the facial reactions shown. As with many viral ads, a series of short scenes is fired out one after the other. Each short scene consists of a different emotion. As soon as the scene is done, a facial expression is shown to reinforce the intended emotion. The patient falls out the back of the ambulance, and scenes of the observers' faces show disgust. The bad guys with guns arrive and scenes of the observers' faces show fear. Darting back and forth between the scenes of the movie and the corresponding facial expressions creates an efficient transfer of emotion.

Facial expressions are a universal form of body language, and humans are able to detect the emotions of others with remarkable accuracy. The emotional contagion effect works because people will tend to adopt the emotions experienced by those around them.

Where words fail, music speaks

Bob Marley once famously said: 'One good thing about music. When it hits you, you feel no pain.'

Most would agree that music is a powerful force in culture and society – I don't think I've ever met anyone who doesn't like music. Music is often found in advertisements, and almost always found in viral advertisements. In some video ads, the music is one of the main features of the ad, relying on the lyrics to tell the story. In other video ads the music plays in the background. But whichever way it features, music can be a powerful element in the success of viral advertisements since music can create or transfer strong emotions from the movie to the viewer.

The 'hit' Bob Marley is referring to is an intense emotional response to music. But despite decades of experiments, scientists still cannot agree on why music has such a profound effect on people. Some scientists argue that our attraction to music is learned, beginning with the sound of our mother's voices singing to us as infants. Others argue that music is biologically programmed, and that we're hardwired to enjoy music. Interestingly, neuroscientists have some evidence to support this latter theory. They found that primitive areas of the brain including the brainstem are activated when people listen to music. These areas of the brain are normally only activated for instinctive behaviours, which are usually biologically set, like eating. They also found that when people listen to music they enjoy, dopamine is released in the brain.

If music enjoyment is biologically programmed into people it does seem odd. Dopamine is a chemical that's usually only released when people do things necessary for ensuring their genes survive, like eating, sleeping and procreating. You wouldn't normally expect music to be necessary for survival. This is the part scientists haven't really figured out – music appears to play a very important role in our wellbeing, but they're not really sure why.

One study might have come close to solving the mystery. Sarah Earp and her colleagues found that the reward system in the brain is activated for female birds in a breeding state who hear birdsong from male birds, but areas of the brain associated with unpleasantness are activated when the birds hear birdsong from other females (Earp and Maney, 2012). Apparently both birdsong and music activate regions of the brain associated with reward and the evolutionary mechanisms usually associated with reproduction. Her research suggests that early mankind might have used music to attract the opposite sex and procreate. Therefore, music did play an important role in terms of making sure our genes survive and get passed on through the generations. It's an interesting theory, and would explain a lot of things about the power of music!

What we're interested in as marketers is how we can harness the power of music to create sharing. We know that there's a relationship between emotions and sharing – the stronger the emotions, the more likelihood of sharing. So of interest to us is how we can use music to create or enhance strong emotions, and therefore get people to share.

So let's first look at how music makes emotions.

What we know is that the different structural features of music create various emotions, which include tempo, pitch, scale and rhythm (Scherer and Zentner, 2001). Each of these structural features influences which emotions are created by the music.

Tempo is the speed with which the music plays, and affects the arousal aspect of emotion. Arousal is the body's biological response to an emotion.

If your heart is beating faster than normal, you are aroused. People associate fast tempo music with high arousal emotions such as ecstasy and anger. If these are the intended emotions in the movie, you should use a fast tempo. In contrast, low tempo music is associated with low arousal emotions like serenity and sadness.

Music pitch is how high or low the notes in the song are. Low pitches are associated with serious and sad emotions, whereas high pitches are associated with humorous and happy emotions.

The scale of music, whether it's major or minor, is another factor influencing the valence of the emotion activated. Major modes in music are usually associated with happy, and minor modes are associated with sad.

The rhythm of music is the presence of a regularly occurring pattern in a song. When the rhythm is smooth, the emotions activated are usually positive, happy and serene. When the rhythm is rough, the emotions are usually associated with uneasiness, and when the rhythm is irregular, the emotions are usually ecstatic (Gabrielsson and Lindström, 2001).

Other structural features of music known to activate certain emotional responses include melodic appoggiaturas which are associated with tears, harmonies which when changed suddenly can cause shivers, and rhythmic syncopation which can directly increase the listener's heartbeat.

Matching the music to the intended emotions in a movie is important, but not always easy, given there are all these moving parts. It's even more difficult when the song is chosen because of the lyrics, since then you're stuck with the tempo, pitch and scale of the original which might not be correctly matched to the emotions in the storyline. If you're trying to create excitement and awe, then slow music will likely ruin what you're trying to achieve. Matching the structural features of the music to the theme of the movie is key to enhancing the desired emotions.

Budweiser faced this dilemma when they produced the advertisement 'Best Buds' (**https://youtu.be/xAsjRRMMg_Q**) for the 2014 American Superbowl. The ad went viral with 2.5 million shares. The ad tells the story of a farmer who loses his puppy while on a trip to town, and the adventures the puppy has trying to find his own way back to the farm. To emphasise the bond between the puppy and the farmer, the ad plays the song

'500 Miles' (**https://youtu.be/tM0sTNtWDiI**) by Celtic pop band The Proclaimers. Obviously these lyrics are ideally matched to the story being told, as well as being well known and having wide appeal. The problem is that the original song is very upbeat and cheery, whereas the themes and emotions of the advertisement are of sorrow and dismay. To overcome this mismatch, Budweiser recrafted the entire song using a different singer, slowing down the tempo, smoothing out the rhythm, and emphasising the minor chord structure. The result is a perfectly matched song for intended emotions in the story in the ad. The resulting composition enhances the emotions in the ad significantly, since the emotions in the song match the intended emotions in the story.

Memories, music and emotion

Have you ever heard a song on the radio that you haven't heard in a long time, and it transported you back in time, put a smile on your face, and sent you into a nostalgic daydream? Likely the song conjured up some strong memories of sometime in the past, which resulted in an equally strong emotional response. This is exactly the kind of powerful response you want to replicate when planning a viral video ad.

Memories that are tied to important events in the past usually have strong emotions attached to them. The problem is, everyone has different memories, so it's difficult to evoke the same emotion from the same memory. There is however one way around this – memories from people's youth.

Most people over a certain age long to be young again, and for most people memories of their youth hold special significance. It's a powerful thing for marketers to tap into these memories since the resulting emotions are not only strong; they're also pleasant emotions. The best way to get at these memories is to use music.

With music it's relatively easy to conjure up nostalgic memories. Most people, as they get older, will at some point stop listening to new music, and continue listening to music from a certain period in their lives – generally late twenties to mid-thirties. After this age, people tend to 'fix' on a certain period of music.

Nostalgic songs don't activate specific memories, but rather the memories that are evoked are more general in nature. Someone in their late thirties to early forties listening to Nirvana's 'Smells like teen spirit' might be reminded of college dorms, parties and late night studying, rather than a specific moment when they heard the song. This makes nostalgic music ideal for conjuring up emotions, since everyone shares general memories of their youth, even though specific memories differ.

If your target audience is known, then evoking nostalgic memories might be as simple as matching a song to the decade in which they were in their late twenties. However, you should be careful about using newer songs because they're more unpredictable in terms of creating emotions, and sometimes don't evoke any meaningful memories at all. This is because each time a song is heard it creates a 'memory trace', which is a small memory of when the song is heard. Songs that are currently popular and heard through multiple sources multiple times in a week create multiple memory traces. Each new memory trace overlays existing memory traces, which dilutes the neural pathways and connection to the reward system, ultimately removing any pleasure from listening. What this means is that the song stops being nice to listen to. This is that 'not that song again' feeling you've probably experienced at least one time in your life. Using a song in a viral advertisement that is currently popular has far less impact in terms of evoking a strong emotional response because of diluted memory traces.

Memory trace

A structural alteration in brain cells that may form a memory.

> ## Tip
>
> If your target audience is known, evoking nostalgic memories might be as simple as matching a song to the decade in which they were in their late twenties.

There's also a problem when the target audience is young, since there's a higher likelihood the nostalgic song you choose is too fresh in their minds to evoke strong nostalgic reflection, because of their age. One technique used to reduce the memory trace problem is to change certain aspects of the composition, while retaining the basic lyrics and melody. Aspects of the original music such as tempo, pitch, scale and rhythm can be adjusted to match the theme of the story, to great effect. A good example of this is the Budweiser 'Best Buds' commercial discussed earlier in this chapter. The theme of the advertisement is comradeship, loyalty and love ('best buddies'). The music used is '500 miles' by Celtic pop band The Proclaimers. The era of song is well timed in terms of Budweiser's target market – many of whom were youthful when the song was first played on the radio. But the original version of the song is catchy, happy and toe-tapping fun, while the theme of the advertisement is more sombre, making the song and the advertisement a poor match. By slowing down the tempo, creating a smoother rhythm, and emphasising the minor chord structure, the song is different enough to create new neural pathways, but familiar enough to evoke nostalgic reflection through the lyrics.

Strong memories usually conjure up strong emotions. Your goal when producing a video ad destined for viral success should always be to maximise the strength of the emotion, since the strength of the emotion is correlated with the likelihood of the ad being shared. Nostalgic memories are usually strong with emotion since people value memories of their youth. The best way to tap into these emotions is through music.

Dumb ways to die

Can joy make you change your behaviour? According to the results from the 'Dumb ways to die' public service advertisement, it can.

The 'Dumb ways to die' (**https://youtu.be/IJNR2EpSOjw**) superviral to date has an impressive five million shares. It's one of the most viral video advertisements of all time. The ad was produced for Australia's *Metro Trains Melbourne* to promote rail safety in the city. It not only went viral, it also had a dramatic effect lowering train and rail deaths. The number of serious injuries as a result of train-related incidences halved, and the number of near misses dropped by 30 per cent.

The video is actually a cartoon, with a catchy song. It features 21 adorable looking characters who each do progressively more stupid things that lead to their death, such as selling both kidneys online, taking their helmet off in space, or dressing up as a moose during hunting season. The skits are comical, and the music is morbidly cheerful. The last of the 'Dumb ways to die' in the video include standing too close to the edge at a train station, running across rail tracks to get to another platform, and driving around boom gates at a level crossing. As the song points out, quite possibly the dumbest ways to die!

'Dumb ways to die' creates a metaphor by using humour and joy to replace the fear tactics usually featured in public service announcements. Nobody likes being told what to do, and shocking people often isn't effective because people believe it will happen to someone else not them. Using metaphors is an effective way to change people's beliefs, by removing the bias and pre-existing assumptions people have. Change people's beliefs and you can change their behaviour.

The power of mixed emotions

Have you ever had a moment of panic when you realised your wallet or phone wasn't where it usually is? Perhaps you tapped your back pocket and felt it wasn't there, or checked inside your bag and couldn't find it. Then with a sigh of relief you found it and realised it was just in a different place?

Recall the feelings you experienced. Chances are you had a physical jolt of panic that felt like your heart skipped a beat, followed by a feeling of blushing in the face, followed by a euphoric feeling of relief. What you experienced is a rapid shift between contrasting emotions. When you realised your phone or wallet was missing, you felt fear. This emotion was quickly replaced with joy knowing that you were mistaken. This mixing of emotions creates 'physiological arousal' that activates motives to share.

Physiological arousal

An increase in heart rate and blood pressure in response to an emotional event.

Imagine if emotions were physical objects and you could place them next to each other in a line, with the most negative emotion at one end, and the most positive emotion at the other end. The middle emotion would be no emotion (indifference). All the negative emotions like fear and disgust would be on the left, and all the positive emotions like joy and affection would be on the right. This is called an 'emotions continuum'.

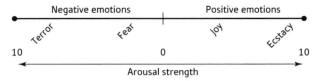

Figure 3.2 Emotions strength continuum

The distance between any two emotions on the emotions continuum is the amount of contrast between the two emotions. The biggest contrast possible would be between the most negative emotion at one end to the most positive emotion at the other end. The greater the contrast between any two emotions on the continuum, the stronger the physiological arousal will be, and therefore the greater the likelihood to share.

Emotions continuum

A theoretical line of emotions, with the most negatively balanced emotion at one end, and the most positively balanced emotion at the other end.

To be effective at creating physiological arousal, emotions must switch between a negative emotion to a positive emotion, or a positive emotion to a negative emotion, in a fast manner. Let's say you were sitting at the roulette table, and you placed a $20 chip on the red number 10. If you had plenty of money, and $20 didn't mean that much to you, then winning would send you from an emotional state of indifference to an emotional state of joy from winning. But it's unlikely this would create a physical response because the distance between the relative indifference to the feeling of joy on the emotion continuum is quite short and doesn't switch between a negative emotion and a positive emotion quickly.

But imagine if the $20 chip was your *last* $20 in the world, and losing would mean you'd have no money for food and would likely be sleeping on the street. If it turns out you won, the physical feeling you'd experience would be far stronger, since your emotions would change rapidly from a feeling of fear (of losing) to joy (of winning). On the emotional continuum, the distance between fear and joy would be far, and cross the line of indifference from negative to positive. As a result, you'd likely experience a stronger physical reaction to winning, including elation and euphoria.

The speed with which the emotions change must be quick. When someone switches from one emotion to another gradually, the physical response is significantly lessened. Imagine if you turned up to work one morning and learned you'd been fired overnight as a result of downsizing. The shock of going from having a job one minute to the fear of being unemployed the next would be great. However, if you had been hearing news reports about impending layoffs beforehand, and listened to rumours from your colleagues that you might be laid off, the stress when the layoff eventually happened would be much less, because the change in emotions would have been more gradual.

The not-for-profit organisation Save the Children produced the viral advertisement 'Most shocking second a day' (**https://youtu.be/RBQ-IoHfimQ**) using mixed emotions. The video has had more than one million shares. It features a series of one-second scenes of memorable moments in a young girl's life. The girl is about ten years old. Each life moment replicates common memories of childhood that anyone would expect to have, such as birthday moments, time spent with family, pets, and play with friends.

The girl's life is one that people are used to living in the western world, with flat screen TVs, music lessons, and an abundance of food choices. The emotions are playful, happy, and joyful.

About 20 seconds into the advertisement, the one-second scenes begin to flash a change in mood as it becomes clear the country the girl lives in is on the verge of war. The scenes switch from times of happiness to times of terror and sadness as the conflict reaches the girl's neighbourhood. The fighting forces her and her family to flee, and after time spent on the run struggling to find food and escape the chaos, she eventually winds up in a makeshift hospital. The scenes are heart-wrenching and full of sadness.

The first scene of the advertisement showed the girl surrounded by smiling friends and family blowing out multiple candles on a pink birthday cake. The last scene shows her alone, blowing out a single candle on something resembling flat bread in a war hospital. It takes one and a half minutes to transport the viewer from the joyful reflection of an innocent girl's childhood, to the terror and despair of war.

Tip

Mix emotions to create a stronger physiological response, and increase motives to share.

The 'Most shocking second a day' video ad emphasised a fast change of emotions by showing a series of one-second scenes. It also switched from positive to negative emotions quickly. This way the advertisement was able to cover a relatively complex story with a sharp contrast of emotions in under one and a half minutes, evoking a physiological arousal response. Not only is this useful for keeping an advertisement brief and holding the viewer's attention, it's also needed for creating the necessary response for activating motives to share.

Karma is feeling

The 'Most shocking second a day' advertisement moved from positive to negative on the emotion continuum. Not-for-profits and charities often use the positive to negative direction because they want the viewer to remember the negative consequences of the cause they support. But for many brands, leaving the viewer on a negative emotion is not ideal. They want to leave the viewer on a positive emotion, since they want people to think positive things about their brand. The problem is that it's more difficult to make the switch from negative emotions to positive emotions work.

The 'Groupon Tibet' (**https://youtu.be/vVkFT2yjk0A**) advertisement was shown during the United States 2011 Super Bowl game. The coveted Super Bowl advertisement spots are guaranteed millions of eyeballs and almost as much attention as the game itself, and are therefore notoriously expensive for advertisers to procure. Many continue to earn thousands and millions of views on YouTube as a result of the initial traction. Unfortunately for Groupon, their advertisement costing over $3 million failed to impress with relatively few views or shares.

The advertisement begins well enough, with majestic scenes of Tibet, its people, and glimpses of a unique culture. The narrator describes how the people of Tibet are in trouble, and the culture is in jeopardy. The scenes evoke sympathy and sadness.

The scenes of Tibet are replaced quickly with a scene of a well-known comedian actor sitting in an American restaurant being served Tibetan food. The actor makes a humorous comment about Tibetan food, and how he and his friends were able to order Tibetan food by using Groupon's services.

The issue with the advertisement is that the switch to the positive emotions using humour is done incorrectly. In this example, the distance between the contrasting emotions was far, and the switch between them was quick, but the physiological response that causes sharing was not activated. The reason is because you cannot easily replace negative emotions with positive emotions, because of the value people place on negative emotions. Generally, the value and strength of negative emotions are stronger than the value and strength of positive emotions, so changing people's emotions from negative to positive is much more difficult than changing their emotions from positive to negative. It's much easier to make a happy person unhappy than it is to make an unhappy person happy.

The 'Groupon Tibet' advertisement failed, because negative emotions are more difficult to change than positive emotions. So how then can you create an advertisement that successfully transitions from negative to positive? The answer lies in *adding* positive emotions to the negative emotions in a synergistic way, not entirely replacing them.

The 'Unsung hero' (**https://youtu.be/uaWA2GbcnJU**) superviral with over one million shares illustrates nicely how to do this. The advertisement was produced by Thai Life Insurance in 2014. It features a man who is seeking good karma in life by doing good deeds others would not normally consider. He notices a leaking pipe on the street, and moves a dying plant to catch the water. He comes across an old lady who is struggling to move her food cart down the street and stops to help her. A hungry stray dog approaches him when he's eating lunch, and he gives the dog his only piece of chicken. He passes a homeless woman and her daughter begging for money on the street, and stops to give them the last of his money.

As the days pass he repeats his behaviour, moving the plant, helping the old lady, feeding the dog, and giving all his spare money to the homeless woman and her daughter. Onlookers shake their heads at his foolishness.

The point of his willingness to help others begins to look questionable as they become more and more dependent on him. But despite the seeming fruitlessness of his efforts, he becomes more and more generous each time as the mood of despair and sadness at mankind's condition deepens.

The movie takes a dramatic turn one day when the man notices the daughter of the homeless woman is no longer with her. The woman is begging alone, and he fears something terrible has happened to her daughter.

Suddenly, from around the corner he hears a girl's voice calling out for her mother. The homeless woman's daughter appears. But she is clean, and dressed in a school uniform clutching a book. He looks back down at the homeless mother, and she begins to smile. She had saved all the money she was given by him to send her daughter to school.

Later on that day he notices the plant he had moved is now green and lush. The old lady with the food cart has become his friend. The dog he feeds has become his pet. He realises he has found karma. Karma is not money or things. Karma is earning the gift of happiness.

It's a beautiful advertisement, and successfully switches from negative emotions to positive emotions. A mood of despair and sadness transitions to a mood of happiness and hope. The transition is successful because the negative feelings of despair and sadness are not discounted or replaced, but rather they are added to. By the end of the movie, the feelings of sadness and despair still exist, but they're complimented, leaving the viewer with a mix of emotions, beginning with negative, and ending with negative mixed with positive.

Changing behaviour using emotions

On my wedding day my father told me that from that day forward I should never criticise my wife's choices, because I was one of them!

Behind his wit was serious advice. From years of experience living in a marriage, he had learnt that criticism comes about because we want other people to do things our way and not theirs. It's a selfish way to live in a marriage, and only ever causes unnecessary arguments. If you want to have a happy marriage he told me, you have to learn to accept other people's way of doing things.

It's common for people to want to change other people's habits and behaviours to suit their own way of doing things. But people generally don't like to change, and that's where the conflict starts. But there are times when it's beneficial for people to change certain behaviours, such as when their behaviour endangers the lives of others, or creates an unfair cost to society.

Drink driving is a behaviour most people want to change. Obviously no one wants to be hit by a drunk driver. When it's a problem to society, the government makes laws and regulations to try and stop people from doing it. But if the behaviour is already embedded in society, then getting people to change their ways requires a different strategy. The most common method used by governments to change prevailing beliefs and behaviours in society is to use a special kind of advertisement called a 'public service advertisement'.

Public service advertisement

An advertisement designed to change an endemic behaviour in society.

The great thing about public service advertisements is that they're usually designed to keep everybody safe, even though some people might disagree with being told what to do. This is in contrast to regular ads that are ultimately designed to make you spend more money. Ironically, it's often easier to get people to spend money then it is to change their behaviour.

The root of the problem with making public service advertisements effective at changing people's behaviour is that people assume bad things will happen to others, and not themselves. Although logically any one of us could be hit by a bus, struck down by illness, or suffer any number of life-threatening experiences at any time, people don't want to believe it will happen to them.

Our minds have evolved over the eons to think positively. It would be abnormal for someone to be constantly worried about their own safety, and would be impossible for someone to be happy if they did so. The stress caused from constant worry would not only be exhausting, it would likely cause physical damage and an early death. So although people remain generally vigilant, people do not tend to dwell on their frailty or mortality. For this reason, public service advertisements that attempt to shock people aren't very effective when it comes to changing their behaviour.

People don't think it will happen to them. The only way for a public service advertisement to have an effect on people is if it changes people's beliefs, since it is people's beliefs that influence their behaviour. Emotions on their own don't change people's beliefs.

The way to change people's beliefs is to make people think about things that matter to them. Thoughts that matter to people almost always come with associated emotions. Rather than making the viewer of your viral ad feel emotions from facial expressions, or music, you make the viewer feel emotions from their own memories. Emotions from meaningful memories can change people's behaviour.

The process that causes an emotional response from memories is internal. This means that it's the person's own memories, not external stimuli that cause people to feel a certain emotion. When people attribute the source of emotion from the self, it can have a stronger effect on behavioural change than if the source of emotion can be attributed to an external event that is less likely to be within someone's control.

One way to activate an emotional response internally from existing memories is to use metaphors. Using metaphors removes the message of the story from its context. This is useful because usually it's the context that causes people to make biased presumptions that lead them to think it won't happen to them. Drink drivers usually think they're better drivers than everyone else, so won't crash when driving drunk. Smokers think they're healthier than they actually are, and so on. By removing the context, people will tend to evaluate the facts in a more objective way.

George Orwell's *Animal Farm* (1945) is an iconic story taught in many schools that's told through metaphors. Given its popularity one could say it's the ultimate viral (technically it's a 'meme' since it's information that gets passed through generations).

Meme

(a) Useful information that gets passed between generations.
(b) An image, text, idea or style that goes viral on the internet.

It tells the story of two pigs at a farm who take over the leadership of the animals after the head pig (Old Major) dies. The two pigs interpret what Old Major's vision for the farm was before he died, and decide to continue his vision. Part of the vision involves taking over the farm from the owner. The whole story is actually a metaphor for the revolution and rise of Stalin in the Soviet Union. Part of the reason for the story's popularity is because it makes people think about an important historical event in a new context. It forces people to form more rational judgements of the events, without the bias introduced from the actual people involved.

'Slap her' (**https://youtu.be/b2OcKQ_mbiQ**) is an Italian superviral, with over two million shares that uses a metaphor to help change behaviour. The movie features five young boys who are given instructions on how to behave in front of a beautiful girl. The movie begins with the narrator asking each of the boys how old they are, and what they hope to be when they grow up. They range in age from 7 to 12, and say they want to be firemen, footballers, bakers, policemen or pizza makers. Then a beautiful girl appears and stands in front of them. The narrator asks each of the boys what they like about the girl, and to tell the girl what they like about her. With much embarrassment each of the boys compliments the girl in his own way. They are then instructed to caress the girl. Again, with much embarrassment they each stroke her hair and face. They're then asked to make the girl laugh. They do so by making a funny face.

Finally, each of the boys is asked to slap the girl.

The boys are visibly shocked at the request, and after moments of disbelief firmly refuse. Their smiles are replaced with looks of confusion. The boys are asked why they refused the instruction to slap the girl, and they explain that it is wrong to hit girls, and that it is wrong to want to hurt her. There's an awkward silence as the boys contemplate what just happened. They move closer to the girl to protect her.

The movie delivers a powerful message against domestic violence by highlighting the flaws in the character of someone who physically abuses women. The emotions evoked by the video are strong in some people, because the emotions are generated from people's existing memories and beliefs. If someone thought violence against women was OK, then they would not feel any emotion. But since most people believe violence against women is wrong, then they feel emotion from their own beliefs about the subject. The strongest emotions would be felt by those people who have been personally affected by domestic violence, and they would be most likely to share the video as a result.

Because the emotions are generated internally from people's existing belief systems, there is more chance that the video ad will be successful in changing behaviour in society. If a violent offender knows that violence against women is wrong, yet uses violence against women, then the guilt and other emotions created by the ad can make them think more seriously about changing or getting help to change. The ad is effective at using internally generated thought processes to evoke an emotional response. Internally generated emotions can be an alternative to creating an emotional response from emotion laden scenes in the actual movie.

When people come across a situation that they've encountered before, they'll think about the emotions the situation made them feel the last time. This will dictate how they deal with the situation. If they felt fear the last time, they'll avoid the situation. If they felt joy the last time, they'll act on the situation. Emotions from the past predict how a person will behave.

People will also predict how others will react to situations based on their own experiences. If someone found something funny, they'll assume everyone else will also find it funny. When people estimate that other people will feel a certain way, and that way is likely to result in gratification, that person will share.

Action plan for using emotion

Emotion is the backbone of viral video ads. When a video ad affects people in a meaningful way, it motivates people to share. The stronger the emotion, the more likelihood that person will share.

When someone watches a video, they estimate what emotions other people will feel when they watch it. They'll share content that creates the emotions they want other people to feel. If something's funny, and they want other people to laugh, they'll share it.

Extra attention should be given to the transfer of emotion. Your video ad might have an ambitious and creative idea, but the emotional reaction to it will be severely diluted if the emotions don't have a way to efficiently transfer to the viewer. An ad that doesn't strongly affect the viewer doesn't get shared.

There are three ways to transfer emotions from the video to the viewer:

1 **Emotional contagion.** Most emotions of interest for marketers have an associated facial expression. People have an impressive ability to recognise emotions from facial expressions, and emotions transferred between people from facial expressions are highly contagious. The best way to transfer emotions from the story using facial expressions is to show short (one- to two-second) scenes of people's facial expressions in the ad reacting to events in the story. Timing is important to reinforce the intended emotion in the story – display the facial expression

immediately after the emotion is cued in the movie, and before the scene is changed or a new spike of emotion begins. Because there are many facial expressions, and the nuances of each can be subtle, it's important you use actors who are well trained on how to mimic the desired facial expressions for each intended emotion in the story. Another way is to use unsuspecting people in an impromptu prank-like storyline, to make the facial expressions genuine.

2   **Music.** Music creates emotions through its structure. Fundamental music structure includes tempo, pitch, scale and rhythm. More advanced compositional structure includes melodic appoggiaturas, harmonies which change suddenly, and rhythmic syncopation. It's important that the structure of the music chosen for your video ad is matched to the intended emotions in the story of the movie. Sometimes, a song might be a perfect choice because of its lyrics, but the structure doesn't match the intended emotions of the storyline. In this situation consider restructuring the song as required, using a different singer to reproduce and sing a matched version. Another issue to be careful about is 'memory tracing'. When a song can be heard from multiple other sources, such as a currently popular song, multiple memory traces overlaying each other can dilute or even eliminate the enjoyment of the song, significantly lowering the effectiveness of an emotional transfer.

3   **Self-evoked emotions.** Another powerful way to transfer emotions is to generate an emotional response through memories. Some memories have more emotion attached to them than others, but because everyone has different memories it's difficult to reliably access only memories with strong emotions. The way around this issue is to target nostalgic memories tied to people's youth. These are easier to access in a wider range of people because they're usually quite general (when people wore grunge clothing) rather than being tied to a specific occasion (the time I was at my friend's party). One way to access nostalgic memories is by using music, since people tend to fix on music from their late twenties to mid-thirties. As an added benefit to transferring emotions using this technique, self-evoked emotions are also more likely to change people's behaviour since they challenge people to re-examine their beliefs. For this reason, self-evoked emotions are the best choice for public service advertisements.

CHAPTER FOUR
Anticipation

Imagine if there were no more surprises in life. If you could see into the future, that's what life would be like. Knowing what and when things were about to happen would eventually become unbearable for many. Uncertainty of things to come is part of what keeps life interesting. Without uncertainty, life would be dull, and there'd be few reasons to live.

Anticipation is the body's response to uncertainty in life. When an upcoming event is a good thing, like a holiday, the feeling of anticipation feels like a yearning. When someone isn't looking forward to an upcoming event, the feeling is more like dread. Whether the anticipation is good or bad, the feelings of anticipation can be just as strong, or sometimes stronger, than the emotions experienced during the actual event.

Why anticipation makes people share

Anticipation is an important part of the story of life, and for that reason it's often found in movies and advertisements that have gone viral. The reason why anticipation causes you to share is because it affects you physically as well as mentally. When people are physically and mentally alert, they tend to be more social, which makes them want to share interesting information with others.

Think about a time in your life when you had a near-miss accident, or some other event that freaked you out. I'll bet you told everyone about it afterwards right? That's because you had an abundance of adrenaline rushing through your system, and had to 'get it off your chest'. The same biological systems that ready the body during a traumatic event also activate when anticipation is strong.

People are also motivated to share when good things happen. When you're looking forward to an upcoming holiday, or planning to move into a better apartment, you just can't help but share the news with others. The reason is also because you're mentally and physically excited.

Fight or flight

Some theorists treat anticipation as an emotion, but it has some unique properties that distinguish it. The first difference is that anticipation occurs before an event, whereas most other emotions typically occur after or in response to an event. Anticipation can also be more prolonged, while most emotions tend to be short lived. The final difference, and perhaps most important, is that anticipation often results in strong physiological effects that mimic primitive survival instincts including fight and flight.

When anticipation is strong it's associated with an increase in physical and mental alertness. The basis of this physiological response stems from ancient survival tendencies. Our ancestors learned long ago that being able to anticipate what was about to happen increased their chances of survival. Imagine walking through a forest filled with predators, completely oblivious to the fact that something could jump out at you at any time and have you for lunch. If you weren't prepared to defend yourself (fight) or run away (flight), your chances of surviving would be slim.

The reason why our bodies physically anticipate a future event ahead of time is because our bodies aren't designed to go from a relaxed state to an energised state prepared to fight or flight very quickly, so anticipation is like a temporary fired-up state in case it's needed. You've probably watched a nature documentary showing a big cat stalking a gazelle without being noticed, and pouncing at the last minute. The attack happens in a flash and is over in a few seconds. If the animal is relaxed and not taking notice, it won't stand a chance. The only chance the animal has of escaping certain death is if the animal is physically and mentally prepared to fight or run away before the big cat attacks.

The human body has adapted over time to stay in a constant state of readiness only when a difficult event is thought to be coming.

Physiological arousal and mental alertness don't have to happen at the same time, and can occur independently of each other. You could be quite relaxed sitting on your couch but be mentally alert watching a documentary on TV. Or you could be physiologically aroused on a treadmill at the gym, but zoned out and dreaming about something far away. It's

Figure 4.1   Source: © Ryan Ladbrook/ Shutterstock.com

important to note that anticipation is associated with someone being both physiologically aroused and mentally alert at the same time.

Anticipation is designed to ready the body for one of two things. Either you'll fight when you meet danger, or you'll run. Both of these reactions require a lot of energy. The body primes itself by releasing adrenaline, which increases the heart rate and prepares the body for physical and mental action. When your body is primed like this you have an urge to be physically active to use up the energy that has been released. Part of this reaction is that it makes people want to be more social. When you're in a condition of anticipated readiness, you experience a greater urge to communicate with others and be social, and you'll also have more confidence. This physical response causes us to be social and share.

Why people can't help looking at blood and guts

'Pub loo shocker' (**https://youtu.be/TADO4LG29bs**) is a superviral that at the time of writing has over 12 million views on YouTube. The advertisement is a public service advertisement about the dangers of driving while drunk. The ad features a prank that's played out in a pub bathroom. Men enter the bathroom, do their business, and as they're washing their hands the realistic head of a body unexpectedly crashes through the bathroom mirror from behind, like someone would smash against their windshield in a car accident. The men are clearly shocked, with reactions ranging from falling backwards, to running out the door. The experience of the advertisement is similar to that experienced in a horror movie – anticipation, some fear, and perhaps disgust.

Usually we would expect videos that create positive emotions to have a better chance of being shared than videos that create negative emotions, since people want to share positive experiences, and don't want to make other people feel bad by sharing negative emotions. Yet the 'Pub loo shocker' video ad did get shared and went viral. Why?

To understand why people share content that creates anticipation and fear, we need to understand the biological basis of these feelings. Anticipation and fear tend to be comparatively strong, and will therefore tend to trigger a physiological response. This physiological response has two distinct elements. The first is arousal, which leads to bodily changes such as heart rate and blood pressure. The second is mental alertness, which increases wakefulness and vigilance. The strength of anticipation and fear can vary. Fear for example could result in a strong physiological response (terror) or a weak physiological response (apprehension). The physiological effects of experiencing anticipation and fear can involve several regions of the brain, including the dopaminergic system which releases dopamine. Someone who rides a rollercoaster might experience terror, but afterwards feel euphoric as a result of the dopamine.

Viral content usually creates a strong emotional response, but it's not the arousal that causes the sharing, rather it's the mental alertness. Content that increases someone's wakefulness and alertness is shareable because wakefulness and alertness are entertaining. It's the opposite of boredom. People have a tendency to want to share entertaining things that increase mental alertness with others, regardless of whether the emotion is negative or positive.

The magic three: humour, awe and thrills

Anticipation is an important sharing motive, and can manifest itself in several ways, though the end result of physiological and mental affects are the same. Anticipation can exist alongside other emotions, notably humour, awe and thrills.

Humour is amusement that sometimes leads to laughter. But how humour creates anticipation is less obvious. When a comedian begins to tell a joke, we find ourselves guessing what the punchline might be. If we guess the punchline before the comedian reveals it, the joke flops. But if the punchline comes as a clever surprise, we find it entertaining. A joke that we know the answer to is rarely funny. People feel anticipation when waiting for the punchline of a humorous situation because they've learned from past experience that the surprise will likely be entertaining. Funny things are pleasurable, so we anticipate something good will happen. Creating a humorous situation relies on anticipating an unexpected surprise.

Awe is more difficult to describe, though if you've ever stood on the edge of the Grand Canyon you'll know what it feels like. Awe has been described as a mixture of fear and wonder. Evolutionary scientists think awe developed from a primeval response to high status people who hold positions of power, such as Kings or Emperors. In order to preserve social hierarchy, and therefore harmony, people felt in awe of those who were powerful. This explains why people feel awe when they see someone who's famous. It also explains why people will pay to see a band play in real life rather than the convenience of simply listening to the album. Awe is the wonderment we feel in the presence of greatness.

Like humour leads to laughter, awe also manifests itself physically. People who are in awe usually have their mouth slightly open, and their eyes open wide. This is the same physical response to a fight or flight situation – the eyes open wide in mental alertness and the mouth opens to facilitate oxygen intake needed to feed the muscles for fight or flight.

The third emotion is thrills, which can best be described as the feeling of goosebumps or chills you feel when something moves you emotionally. Perhaps you've had a feeling of chills or shivers when listening to a certain part of a song, or when someone physically attractive has touched you. If an event has ever made the hairs on the back of your neck stand up, then most likely you were experiencing thrills.

Tip

Anticipation can also be created by using humour, awe and thrills in video footage.

In viral advertising, attempts to make something thrilling are common. Red Bull and GoPro are two brands that frequently use thrills in extreme sports type advertisements. One of the more effective examples is the

'GoPro backflip over 72-ft canyon' (**https://youtu.be/x76VEPXYaI0**) super-viral with close to one million shares. The superviral features point-of-view footage of freeride mountain biker Kelly McGarry riding his bike across a narrow rocky ridge. At the end he pulls a harrowing backflip. With the point-of-view perspective, the ride is truly thrilling. The transfer of the thrill is achieved by shooting the footage from the perspective of the rider. The video gives the viewer an insight into what it is like to be a mountain bike stunt rider, and because of the point-of-view footage, the thrills experienced by the rider transfer to the viewer.

Action plan for anticipation

When thinking about a viral idea, it's important to consider how to maximise physiological arousal, since physiological arousal activates motives to share. One way to create physiological arousal is by creating strong anticipation.

In this chapter, I described three emotions that each can co-exist with anticipation: humour, awe and thrills. It's important when considering how to create anticipation that each of these emotions is strong enough. Furthermore, it's important that the transfer of these intended emotions is effective. Superior creativity is often required to ensure the story can create strong enough humour, awe and thrills. But even with the best talents, the effectiveness of the intended emotions can be significantly weakened or even lost if the emotions aren't sufficiently transferred to the viewer.

The best way to transmit these emotions is to include an actor in the story who experiences these emotions in a strong way. The transfer of the emotion to the viewer then occurs through social contagion, either from a point-of-view camera technique, or from the facial expressions of the actors in the movie. One of the factors that makes the thrill effect so strong in the 'GoPro backflip over 72-ft canyon' advertisement is that it's shot from the perspective of the rider. When watching the ride, the viewer is able to feel more closely what the rider must have been feeling. Because the footage is shot from a point-of-view perspective, the viewer is able to feel what it would have been like as the actor, rather than as an observer. Through emotional contagion, the thrill transfers to the viewer more effectively.

5

Affinity

Jack was born in a small rural town hospital in Western Australia in 1973. His father owned a modest-sized cattle farm, and his mother bred Australian cattle dogs which she sold. Like many farms in the Australian outback at the time, motorbikes had largely replaced horses as a mode of transport. Jack loved riding on the back of his father's motorbike along the thin red dirt tracks spanning the land.

Motorcycling is popular in Australia, largely because of the temperate year round climate, an abundance of 'twisty' roads, and a rural culture where motorcycles are an important part of outback transport. Many Australians start riding at an early age, and it's not uncommon for young Australians to be expert motorcycle riders before they're even able to drive a car.

By the time Jack was nine, he was nagging his father to buy him his own motorbike. His best friend and neighbour Derek had one, and they had plans to race each other and build a dirt track. So on his tenth birthday, despite his mother's protests, Jack's father bought him an 80cc two-stroke Suzuki.

Jack spent hours on his new toy, from the moment he got home from school until sunset he zoomed round and round the paddocks, and up and down the red dirt tracks. At the weekends, his friends arrived early with shovels, and they would spend half the day digging jumps and berms, and the other half doing hair-raising jumps and racing. Jack's father even helped them to build a race track with his digger. Jack's mother couldn't bear to watch, and tended to her dogs.

The better Jack got at drifting around corners and flying through the air, the more competitive he got, and it wasn't long before Jack was spending his Sundays racing at the district motocross meets. By the time Jack was 14 he was already competing in the 250cc class with men much older than him, and his father's mantelpiece was cluttered with trophies. In the local motocross scene, Jack was a celebrity.

By the time Jack was 18, he had completed his schooling, and had found a job as a farmhand on a ranch 40 miles on the other side of town. Jack's passion for motorcycles had broadened, and by that age many of Jack's friends had moved on from dirt bikes to road bikes and cruisers. Following his friends, Jack sold his dirt bike and bought an old Harley-Davidson Sportster.

Riding a road bike was slightly more boring than riding a motocross bike, but had the added benefit of making Jack look cool and impressing more girls. As he grew older Jack found himself more likely to be hanging out in a friend's garage listening to music and drinking beer than down at the motocross meet winning races. Gone were the flashy armour and full faced helmets of his motocross youth. Jack wore ripped jeans, a leather jacket, engineer boots, and a variety of tattoos.

There's nothing like the feeling of riding down an open highway he told himself. For Jack, riding a motorbike was all about freedom.

Jack's motorcycle shop

One thing that hadn't changed between Jack and his friends was their shared interest in bike mechanics. As youngsters they never had enough money to pay a mechanic to service their dirt bikes, and so they learned how to do it themselves. Motocross bikes take a fair thrashing, and Jack was quite used to stripping down his bike and installing new shocks, brakes, bars and controls, rims and tyres. Jack's new Harley was no different, and there was nothing Jack loved more than ordering something new, installing it, and showing his friends.

Jack's passion for customising his bike was expensive, and the pleasure of buying something new was tempered with the anxiety of having to save up his meagre wages. He had his eye on a bigger and better bike, and numerous aftermarket parts, but he couldn't bear to wait. So Jack spent his nights lying alone in bed planning how he could earn more money to satisfy his need to buy motorbikes. The solution he concluded was simple – he had to own his own motorcycle shop.

Jack quickly discovered that starting a business was not as easy as it sounded. The first problem was start-up capital. He applied for a loan at the bank, but they refused. But in a strange coincidence of grief and fortune, soon after his loan application was refused, Jack's grandfather Jack Senior passed away. Jack had no idea his grandfather had any money, and was surprised to learn he had inherited enough to purchase a lease on a medium-sized store in town, some stock, and some tools. Jack briefly considered spending the money on a new motorbike and holidays, but soon dismissed the idea. By that stage Jack had already convinced himself that he needed a shop. He was tired of working for someone else, and was looking forward to the dignity of owning his own business.

Jack's dream had finally come true. In honour of his grandfather, 'Jack's Motorcycles' began trading in August 2003, exactly 20 years since his father gave him his first motorcycle for his birthday.

Affinity, and the art of building an iconic brand

I first met Jack in Japan when I was on a skiing holiday. We were staying at the same lodge, and since we were both travelling alone we often skied together and ate at the same restaurant. We got on pretty well, and kept in touch. Jack sometimes came to Melbourne to visit one of his suppliers, where we would catch up for lunch or a beer.

One day I got a call from Jack. He was coming to Melbourne, and wanted to go out for a drink. I arranged to meet him at a local pub.

I arrived at the pub early, and waited by the window. Jack was late, but I finally spotted him walking down the street. As Jack walked through the door with his head down, I could sense something was wrong. I bought him a beer, and before Jack could get the next round I asked him if something was bothering him.

He began to explain his woes. Selling new motorcycles was tough. Jack had dreams of selling the kinds of motorcycles he'd like to own himself. But the reality was that he was selling mostly farm bikes to local farmers, and spending all his time doing repairs. Jack's dream was barely surviving, and things were about to get even worse. A franchise motorcycle dealer from Sydney had just opened up a shop in his town, and word had got around that Jack's prices were too high. The franchise had the buying power that Jack simply couldn't compete against. He was losing money, and about to lose his business.

Jack knew a lot about motorcycles, but not about business. He had put a 'Sale' banner on his front window, which was now faded and was starting to look like a permanent fixture. He dropped his prices as far as he could, but it was no use. Jack was going broke, and he had no idea how to fix it.

Competing on price is never a good idea, and I was convinced Jack needed to focus on building his brand. There was no use going head-to-head with his competitor, Jack simply didn't have the resources to compete using that kind of strategy. We put our heads together and started to plan.

We sat in the pub until closing time. I looked at his website, his competitor's website, and discussed the details of his marketing efforts. Basically Jack purchased radio advertisements from time to time, and usually had a small advertisement in the local newspaper. His advertisements were focussed on new models he had in, or his repair and maintenance services. I needed to get Jack to think about building a brand, not selling bikes.

The focus of Jack's marketing was on the tangible features of motorbikes – the brands, models, specs, sizes, and of course prices. Jack was the most enthusiastic motorcyclist I knew, but since I'd known him I'd never heard him tell me about the price of his own motorcycle, or even what type of motorcycle it was. Jack's motorcycle stories were always about his experiences – adventures, people he met on the road, morning rides through the mountains, and the comradeship of his motorcycle buddies. I asked Jack to remind me: 'Jack, what's the attraction of riding a motorcycle?'

He didn't answer right way, but instead turned his head and gazed out the window. He sighed. After a long pause he mumbled, 'There's nothing like the freedom of riding a motorcycle. Nothing.'

I waited, and then told him, 'Well Jack – ever since I've known you all you've talked about are your motorcycling adventures, but I've never heard you talk about how much you paid for your bike, what model it is, or even what colour your bike is. Why do you think that is?' It took a moment, then Jack finally turned his head towards me. Slowly his face lit up, he wiped his eyes with his sleeve, and that big cheesy smile returned. He straightened his back and in a loud voice he exclaimed, 'Freedom and lifestyle! That's it!' The barman looked over. Jack turned towards him and explained with passion: 'People don't care about how powerful their motorcycle is, or what colour it is, and how much it costs. Riding a motorcycle is about freedom and life-style!' The barman's head turned to one side as he assessed the drunkenness of my friend. Jack slapped me on the back and headed for the bathroom, grinning from ear to ear.

Jack realised from that point on that what really mattered to his customers was how motorcycling made them feel. It wasn't all about the machine, it was about the culture and the experience. That's where the real value was, and that's how he decided to position his brand.

What Jack had discovered was something called 'affinity'. Affinity is that feeling you get when you think about something you love. People experi-ence affinity for the way objects, activities, or even ideas make them feel. Motorcycle enthusiasts love their lifestyle because of the culture, the feel-ing of freedom and excitement, the thrill-seeking sense of adventure, and the fraternity of membership with other motorcyclists. People like their motorcycles too, but it's the feeling the motorcycle experience gives them that really matters.

Over the next 12 months I helped Jack reconfigure his marketing strategy, but I could tell that Jack was very capable of turning it around himself. We designed an online marketing campaign around an image of a man in his forties wearing a bandana, leaning back on a classic Indian motorcycle on a deserted outback high-way. The image reeked of freedom and cool, and was designed to directly align with a segment we identi-

Affinity

A feeling of warmth, respect and deep appreciation for an activity, idea or object.

fied as having the most disposable income and frequency of purchase: men between the ages of 35 and 50. We used a humorous tagline: 'If you want to be happy for a day, drink. If you want to be happy for a year, marry. If you want to be happy for a lifetime, come to Jack's Motorcycles!' The focus of the campaign was on the lifestyle of riding and not the motorcycle itself, as it had been in the past.

Jack rearranged his shop, moving some of his custom motorcycles to the display front, with pop culture memorabilia from the classic café racer culture of England and the long haul cruiser culture of the Americas adorning the window displays and walls. He installed red leather couches, started selling coffee and beverages, and convinced a local collector to lease him some of his classic rare motorcycles to display on his shop floor. His shop began to look like a cross between a motorcycle museum, and a café from the 1960s.

Jack invited motorcycle tourers who had accomplished amazing tours through exotic countries to give free talks in the evenings, and organised 'Poker Run' group rides in the weekends, all sponsored by Jack's Motorcycles. It was hard work, but it payed off. Jack's sales grew slowly, as his shop's reputation changed from being known as an expensive place to buy a motorcycle, to an iconic motorcycle experience that was cool to visit.

Jack's focus on the experience and culture of riding was a legendary success. Jack lost most of his old local farmer clients to the franchisee, but gained a wealthy and loyal customer base of hard core motorcycle enthusiasts from all over the state. Jack even tells me he now has tourists stopping by to see his shop and that he makes more money selling 'Jack's Motorcycle Shop' t-shirts in a month than he used to make servicing motorcycles in a year.

Jack, the farm hand from Western Australia, had just built the foundations of an iconic brand.

Affinity vs. emotion: what's the difference?

Affinity is a powerful feeling that creates the foundations of sharing. Affinity manifests itself as a feeling of warmth, respect or deep appreciation for an activity, idea or object. Affinity is different from emotion for several reasons.

An emotion is characterised by some kind of physiological effect. Adrenaline is released, and blood pressure increases. Facial expressions might change to match the emotion. Emotions are characterised by energy and a physical change in the body. They're usually short term, and can come and go quickly.

Affinity in contrast is a long-term quality of feeling. It is a passion that somebody has for something that radiates from the heart. It is a closeness to something, characterised by passion.

Operationally, affinity has greater importance for the prediction of viral content than emotion.

When annoying the neighbours is shareable

Marshall Amps circulated a picture meme on Facebook in 2013. There were two versions of the exact same picture, though they were released months apart. The picture was of the top section of the infamous Marshall Stack guitar amplifier. This particular amplifier holds special significance for those who play electric guitar since it's associated with the world's most iconic guitar legends including Jimi Hendrix, Pete Townshend and Jimmy Page, to name a few. Marshall Amps was all about playing loud, and that resonates with those who play rock. In fact, there's a strong association between Marshall and loudness for guitar players – Marshall is known for being the first to produce a 100-watt amp that could be heard above the crowd when bands started playing in stadiums.

Figure 5.1
Source: © Andrew Spiers/
Alamy Stock Photo

There was a difference between the two pictures. On the first version just below the picture it said: 'Marshall Amps. Since 1962'. It earned around a hundred 'Likes', and about 40 'Shares'. On the second version, released months after the first, it said: 'Pissing off the neighbours since 1962'. This one earned almost 80,000 'Likes' and an impressive 27,000 'Shares'. This one had obviously gone viral.

You might be thinking that the message on the second image was perhaps more amusing, and therefore it was shared more because the emotion was stronger (see **Chapter 3** on emotion). But this isn't the whole explanation.

There's a more important difference between them that explains why one went viral. The second image creates 'time-based affinity'.

People who played electric guitar when they were young know exactly what it was like to annoy the neighbours by playing too loud. The second image reminds guitar players of a time when they were young and free. People's memories of their youth have special significance for them because it was when they were their best looking, and had opportunities and their life ahead of them. People feel strong affinity for those times. Marshall Amps created affinity by activating meaningful memories from a time that matters to people. In doing so, it created a desire to share the image.

In contrast to the second image that went viral, the first image reminds people of the brand's heritage: 'Marshall Amps. Since 1962'. The statement possibly creates affinity for long-term employees of the company, but it's difficult to see how it could have the same meaningfulness for Marshall's customers. It doesn't create affinity because for most people it's simply a fact about the brand.

So how does time-based affinity lead to sharing? According to scientists who've researched in this area, there's a connection between meaningful memories and relationship building.

Clay Routledge and his colleagues did a study to understand how memories from the past impacted people's behaviour in the future (Routledge *et al.*, 2011). Their study found that thinking about meaningful events in the past elevates a person's mood and boosts their self-esteem, and that sharing meaningful events that happened in the past strengthens relationships. This explains why much of our conversation is about events that have happened in the past. Next time you have a conversation with someone, try to only use the present tense. It's much more difficult than you think!

Time-based affinity

Feelings of warmth, respect and deep appreciation towards activities, ideas or objects, activated from meaningful memories.

Another theory proposed by Constantine Sedikides and his colleagues from the University of Southampton suggests that people share meaningful memories with others to give them a sense of meaning and purpose in life (Sedikides *et al.*, 2008). They found that people use time to help justify their existence and convince themselves that their lives have meaning. People share memorable moments in their lives with others as a way to remind themselves that they have meaning and purpose. I suppose this explains why people like showing each other photographs of their holidays.

Understanding how affinity is linked to time is important for marketers because time-based affinity is a driver of rapid and sustained sharing. When you feel affinity with something, it feels like a sense of longing. It radiates from the heart. But it's not always possible to activate this feeling in your target audience for something they love right now. Chances are that most of them do care about memories from their youth. Time-based affinity uses memories to activate affinity, which has wider effectiveness than current affinity.

Oh, boy!

One thing that a lot of people remember from their youth is Disney. When I was young I loved watching the Disney cartoons, and there was nothing I wanted more than to visit Disneyland. It wasn't until I had kids of my own that I finally had the chance to go to Disneyland, but taking my kids there made it even more special.

In early 2015 Disney Parks produced a prank movie played out in a mall. Disney's 'Oh, boy!' (**https://youtu.be/Hd_2Y29_FLU**) soon went viral, and at the time of writing it has 3.6 million shares. The movie features a fictitious magic shop in a mall that looks like it's new and has yet to open. The shop has white opaque screens covering the windows. But as unsuspecting passers-by walk by the shop, magic happens.

As people walk by, a shadow of a Disney character on the other side of the screen mimics them walking. Some people stop and make random movements to play along with the mimicking. Others dance with the characters, revealing remarkable dexterity from the mimickers. Both adults and children get involved. Each person gets a different Disney character. Goofy, Mickey, Cinderella and Buzz Lightyear all feature. Each experience is as surprising as it is entertaining. After a crowd is drawn the prank ends with the Disney characters revealing themselves from behind the screen.

Many people have strong memories of Disney from their youth, and like the Marshall picture meme described earlier in this chapter, youthful memories are full of meaning and can evoke strong affinity. The Disney movie accesses youthful memories and therefore uses time-based affinity.

The Disney 'Oh, boy!' video illustrates something important about how affinity motivates people to share. Affinity is not a reason for sharing, but rather it's a fundamental requirement for sharing. If a video or image doesn't have affinity it won't get shared. Affinity is required to create a motive to share. The Marshall Amp advertisement also activates time-based affinity, but it's likely the reason for sharing is based on self-enhancement motives. Recall from **Chapter 2** on self-enhancement that people will often share content with others to signal something about their identity. Guitar players might share guitar-related content to signal to others something about their personality or character, or to signal legitimacy of membership. In contrast, the Disney 'Oh, boy!' video sharing is more likely motivated by a desire to bond with family and children. People like sharing entertaining things because it makes them look like an interesting person, but people also have a natural desire to be social and form relationships with others, which goes beyond simply signalling to others something about their identity. The Disney 'Oh, boy!' video demonstrates how creating time-based affinity in a video ad can influence the success of sharing.

First kiss

Tatia Pilieva used to keep a folder on her computer entitled 'kisses'. Inside was a collection of photos of her and her husband kissing in different places around the world over a nine-year period. Whenever she was feeling sad and down, she would open the folder and look at the photos. They made her feel better.

One day she had a crazy idea. What would happen if you put two strangers together and asked them to kiss? Not just a peck on the check, but a full-on kiss on the lips!

She handed the task of filming over to her husband Andre, and with the help of her friend recruited 20 willing participants. She arranged for everyone to meet at the same location, paired the couples together, and began to film. With awkwardness, 20 people passionately kissed someone they had only just met.

After filming, Tatia posted her film on Style.com, YouTube, and Vimeo. Within two hours the film earned 200 views. By evening it had exploded to 600,000 views. When she woke up the next day it had five million views. At the time of writing, 'First kiss' (**https://youtu.be/IpbDHxCV29A**) has over 100 million views.

'First kiss' uses affinity, but in a different way. Obviously most people care about sexual relations – procreational tendencies are biologically programmed into us. But the movie isn't sleazy in any way – rather it radiates more of a romantic vibe. The scenes in 'First kiss' are of situations that almost no one has ever encountered themselves. No one starts kissing a stranger moments after they've just met. But at the same time the idea is probably quite appealing to many. So the affinity is not really generated from memories, rather, it's generated from an ideal of what could be.

I believe that in this case, 'First kiss' has generated affinity from instinctual desires. Although the movie begins quite awkwardly, the theme appears to be more centred on the ideal of romance, which is an appealing theme in classic storytelling that has stood the test of time. People place great importance and meaning on storytelling, and despite some awkwardness, the movie manages to create an ideal that is appealing to a wide section of society. In an interesting way, 'First kiss' is successful at creating affinity by activating some people's ideals of romance and story.

World's toughest job

The 'World's toughest job' (**https://youtu.be/HB3xM93rXbY**) video is a superviral with over two million shares. The video features a prank whereby a fictional company interviews potential employees for the position of Operations Manager. When describing the requirements of the job, the interviewer tells the candidates that they must be willing to stand up most of the day, and be on call 24 hours. The candidates are perturbed, but remain interested and continue to present themselves in the best light. The interviewer then tells them that they should expect no scheduled breaks, and be prepared to work extra hard on public holidays including Christmas and Thanksgiving. The candidates start to look worried, but persevere. Finally, the interviewer tells the candidates that they must be willing to do the job for free. By this stage of the interview the candidates are shocked, telling the interviewer the job sounds cruel, inhumane, unfair, and potentially illegal.

The video concludes with the interviewer letting the interviewees in on the prank. He explains that there are already many billions of people throughout the world who are doing the exact same job: mothers.

The 'World's toughest job' video is an example of a video that has gone viral without creating any significant emotions, though it does create affinity. It's like a riddle – a series of obscure clues that eventually leads to an 'a-ha' moment. Like some of the other examples in this chapter, the movie uses time-based affinity by activating existing memories. Most people obviously have rather powerful memories of their mother, and by placing the focus on work, the video successfully creates a feeling of appreciation towards mothers. This feeling is important to people, and memories of our mothers bringing us up are strong and have special meaning. Affinity is necessary for something to go viral, but it doesn't need emotions to work.

Can gift giving cause sharing?

Almost everyone has happy memories of giving and receiving gifts in their lives. But are these memories meaningful enough to create a sense of affinity? As this next example shows, it depends on when the video is watched, and something called 'tip-of-mind'.

Tip-of-mind

A thought that is easily accessible because of recent and frequent activitation.

'WestJet Christmas miracle' (https://youtu.be/zIEIvi2MuEk) is a superviral with 2.2 million shares that came out in December 2013. The video features a kiosk set up in an airport lounge with Santa Claus on screen asking passengers what they want for Christmas before they board their flight. People tell Santa what they want, assuming the kiosk is a novelty entertainment gimmick, before rushing off to catch their flight. What the passengers aren't aware of is that as soon as they board the plane, the staff of the airline rush to purchase the gifts the passengers asked for. When the passengers arrive at their destination and make their way to the luggage carrousel to collect their bags, they're surprised to find Christmas wrapped boxes coming out instead of suitcases. Each wrapped box has a label on it with a passenger's name, and inside each box is the gift each passenger asked for when interacting with the Santa Claus kiosk. The passengers are delighted, and the kindred spirit of Christmas brings everyone in the room together in a moment of shared joy.

Like many of the other examples in this chapter, the 'WestJet Christmas miracle' video creates affinity by activating memories. In this case, the sense of affinity comes from feelings of receiving and giving gifts. But this in itself might not create sufficient affinity for a wide audience, if it weren't for the fact that the video was shown during the Christmas period.

One thing that can boost the meaning and importance of thoughts is tip-of-mind. When something is thought about often, it has more meaning. The 'WestJet Christmas miracle' video was filmed when the Christmas spirit was in full swing. Cues of gift giving would have been all around and therefore everyone would have had frequent thoughts about gift giving. Because the thoughts of gift giving would have been recent and frequently activated from gift giving cues, the idea of gift giving would have been tip-of-mind for everybody. As a result, the idea of gift giving would have had more importance, and had more affinity, than if the video were shown during a time in the year when cues of gift giving were infrequent.

Affinity is more than activating motives to share. It's also about reminding your customers why they should care about your brand. The ultimate aim for any marketer should be to create a warm feeling that radiates from the heart. That's affinity.

Jack's Motorcycle Shop demonstrates how affinity can be used to build favourable associations with the brand. At every touchpoint, from the t-shirts, to the experience of the store, to the organised events, Jack's customers are reminded of why they love the culture of motorcycling. Jack positioned his brand as an 'enabler' of the motorcycle passion. Using affinity helped Jack to create a sense of community and belonging with his customers. I believe that if Jack were to go out of business now, he would actually break a lot of hearts! How many businesses can say that?

When people think about Jack's shop they *feel* something – that's the ultimate goal for any brand. It's more than recognition and recall of your brand through advertising; the real value of a brand is how much your customers care about you. People love Jack's Motorcycle Shop, and Jack's Motorcycle Shop loves its customers. What is Jack's advice to others when he is asked about his success? 'Love your customers, and they'll love you back.'

Action plan for affinity

Affinity is a feeling of warmth, respect, and deep appreciation for an activity, idea or object. Affinity is different from emotion, which is characterised by a more short-term physical response to a stimulus. Affinity is an enduring quality of feeling radiating from the heart, that doesn't necessarily have any physical symptoms, nor is it short term. Although Jack's Motorcycle Shop showed that affinity can be used to create positive associations for a brand, it's most often a feature that contributes to motives to share in branded video ads.

The most important thing to note about affinity is that it's a requirement for something to go viral. If somebody doesn't relate to or care about your marketing, then they most certainly won't share it. Although emotion might be important when creating marketing content, affinity is critical.

One of the ways to create affinity is to remind people why they love something. The biggest problem with this however is that not all of your target audience might like the same thing. It's of course easier if you're selling something where your target market is bound together by a shared passion, like motorcycling, but for many brands their target audience is more mixed. In this situation, activating meaningful memories that a wider range of people care about is a better choice.

So-called 'time-based affinity' creates a sense of warmth from memories that have meaning. This chapter described two sources of time-based affinity:

1   **Youth.** Most people value memories from their youth. Activating time-based affinity from youth-based memories requires finding a memory theme that has strong meaning from when people were young. Memories from youth don't have to be specific memories, but rather can be characterised by themes, which widens their appeal. For example, everyone has memories of receiving gifts in their youth, or the magic of Disney. These memories are tied to nostalgic times of being young, which do have importance for a wide range of people.

2 **Relationships.** Almost everybody has had relationships in their lives that matter to them. Again, these memories can be of a general nature (e.g. mothers, rather than a specific person), and therefore are easier to activate in a meaningful way to a wider range of people. Using this strategy, your task should be to identify a likely relationship situation that matters, which usually means romantic or family based, but could also be mentor based, such as a teacher or leader.

Finally, to boost the effectiveness of time-based affinity, tip-of-mind memory cues should be used. The most obvious way to do this is to base your choice of memory being accessed on a current event. For example, if you're trying to access motherhood memories, then the release of your viral content would be most effective in the days leading up to Mother's Day.

Do *not* under any circumstances try to use 'negative affinity', which means 'riding the wave' of people's affinity towards the pain and suffering caused by a current disaster. When a human disaster is trending on the news or Twitter, it is wise to cease all marketing communications immediately. Brands who attempt to use negative affinity caused by a current disaster will likely suffer an uncontrollable negative backlash and possibly irreparable damage against their brand. Though it might be tempting to choose negative affinity, it is wiser to always choose positive affinity.

6

CHAPTER SIX
Justice

Chris lived in a poor neighbourhood in Brooklyn, New York. His mother was a teacher and social worker for the mentally handicapped, and his father drove a truck. To give Chris a better chance in life, Chris's parents enrolled him into a school in a wealthier part of town. This meant a very long commute, but that wasn't what Chris most despised. Chris was the only African American at his school, and because of his ethnicity he was bullied.

The abuse Chris suffered was appalling – he was beaten, spat on, and even one day had balloons filled with urine thrown at him. Worse, the abuse wasn't confined to his fellow students. Chris recalled a group of parents rallying outside his school one day holding picket placards with 'n****r go home' written on them. It was 1977.

Because of the bullying, Chris dreaded going to school each day. The bus ride in each morning was wrought with anguish. All he could think about was the abuse he would suffer. Then one day Chris had an idea. He had to protect himself, and decided he would do something the bullies wouldn't be expecting. He walked into his classroom before class was about to start, and took his seat. He took a deep breath, composed himself, and belted out a self-deprecating remark about African Americans. Everybody stopped talking. There was a look of astonishment as faces turned towards Chris. After a moment's silence Chris made a loud joke about himself. Cautiously, someone began to giggle. This time Chris stood up, and made a joke about his mother being a cheapskate. The giggles turned to laughter. The boys in his class who usually bullied him looked amused. That day, Chris didn't get bullied.

As the weeks passed Chris thought up new material to stave off his attackers. For Chris, comedy became his protection blanket. As long as he was making people laugh, life was more bearable. Chris diversified and tried jokes not only about his ethnicity, but also about parents, relationships and music. Sometimes he earned laughs, sometimes he didn't. What was important to Chris was that he was learning what worked and what didn't. Chris the joker could cope with life, but the real Chris was someone people despised. Being the joker gave him the freedom to express himself, and a way to distance himself from his tortured soul.

Chris eventually left his school, and plucked up the courage to try stand-up comedy at the 'Catch a Rising Star' comedy club in New York. He arrived when it opened at 7.45 pm, and left at 2 am in the morning. Over the course of six years doing stand-up at CRS, he studied other comedians religiously. Chris realised the secret to becoming a great comedian was learning what didn't work, more than what did. He took notes, and got into the habit of observing behaviours that most people took for granted. His style evolved to be unique, edgy and controversial, as he continued to use self-deprecation in his act. Word slowly got around that Chris's act was one not to be missed.

Chris eventually got a break when he was successful in auditioning for the popular sketch comedy series *Saturday Night Live*. He landed his first major film role in *Beverley Hills Cop II* (1987) starring Eddie Murphy, which led to a career in acting, and eventually three Emmy awards including 15 nominations.

In 2001 *Time* magazine named Chris Rock the funniest man in America. (see **http://www.vulture.com/2014/11/chris-rock-frank-rich-in-conversation.html** and **https://en.wikipedia.org/wiki/Chris_Rock**).

Fairness, justice and an unfair advantage

Self-deprecating humour, or making oneself the object of a joke, is one of the most popular strategies used by comedians all over the world. The reason why it works so well is because people have a natural attraction to those who are disadvantaged in an unfair way. The unlikely contestant in the talent show who blows everyone away, or the kid who defeats a bully at school shares the same themes as iconic stories of triumph like Cinderella or David and Goliath. It's actually no surprise that many of the world's most viral stories are based on an underdog theme, because the power of our instinct to support the underdog runs very deep.

The basis of people's desire to support the underdog rests on their sense of fairness and justice. This sense of fairness and justice has an instinctual basis, since our ancestors relied on a harmonious society for survival purposes. This can be very powerful for marketers to take advantage of since obviously brands would like to be the Cinderella in a market, and ads that feature an underdog theme are usually very shareable.

But just because someone is disadvantaged, it doesn't necessarily mean that they will earn people's support. Homeless people for example don't always get the sympathy that some would argue they deserve. Yet someone who is beating the odds to fight an injustice will get enormous support. The fundamental requirement for positioning yourself as an underdog is that you're a weaker entity facing adversity. But even this by itself is often insufficient. Positioning yourself as an underdog is not easy. To turn a disadvantaged person into an underdog, three conditions are necessary.

The first necessary element of a viral underdog story is a degree of distance between the disadvantaged person and the observer. This means that the person viewing the story shouldn't know or have some kind of affiliation with the proposed underdog. You're unlikely to feel your own sports team is the underdog for example. But if it's a team you don't know much about, and the other conditions are in place, then you'll be more likely to develop a passionate desire to see that team win!

The second necessary feature needed to create a viral underdog story is injustice in the form of an *unfair* disadvantage. It is insufficient to create a story whereby the person or group is simply disadvantaged; the disadvantage needs to be clearly unfair.

The third condition necessary for a successful underdog illusion is a clear emphasis on *effort*, not ability. The observer of an underdog must feel that the underdog is deserving, and that they're deserving because of their efforts not just their ability. People will believe someone deserves something only when their actions are perceived as good actions, and when the outcome is also perceived to be good. The difference between effort and ability is that effort is perceived to be under someone's control, but ability is perceived to be not under someone's control. Effort is directly associated with the task at hand, and people who try hard are generally more respected than those who do not try hard but have a capable ability. Therefore, people are more likely to attribute deservingness to effort because it is believed to be under the person's control.

Chris Rock's story is surprisingly similar to many other comedians. What's interesting is how many of them learned to turn the object of their pain into laughs. Chris Farley was bullied as a child because of his weight, and often framed his gags on screen and on stage about being fat. Robin Williams struggled with addiction, and often used the theme of addiction in his gags. One study done on 500 comedians discovered they had an unusually high incidence of psychotic characteristics related to both schizophrenia and depression compared to everyone else. The study concluded that many successful comedians have become good at what they do because they've used humour all their lives to deal with psychological distress. But the one thing that all these comedians have in common is that they've learned how to balance 'unfair advantage' and 'effort over ability' to earn the crowd's support. The best comedians are not only funny, they're also loveable.

The little girls who showed the world

Perhaps the most obvious underdog theme is of a weaker sports team beating a stronger sports team. This is the storyline Powerade chose when they produced the underdog advertisement 'Powerade the dance' (**https://youtu .be/dOoZwLgxOMU**) to compete against the dominant competitor in the sports drink market, Gatorade.

The advertisement features the Powerade basketball team in a locker room being given a pep talk by their coach just before a game. The coach reminds the team that although their opponents may have better resources, gold uniforms, star players, and the crowd on their side, they can 'power through' and triumph.

Unfortunately the advertisement never went viral.

When a fan's sports team is expected to win a game, it doesn't activate the same feelings of fairness and justice as with a true underdog story because the team is already expected to win. Most people know who Powerade is, and the team in the ad is a direct representation of the brand. People would expect Powerade to win since it's a Powerade sponsored ad. This eliminated any possibility of creating an underdog effect, and as a result the advertisement never went viral. For the advertisement to have had a chance to go viral there needed to be complete separation from the sports team depicted in the advertisement and the brand. Using an actual team rather than the fictitious 'Powerade' team would have been preferable.

Another contributing factor preventing the success of the Powerade ad is that the ad doesn't convince the viewer that there is any injustice in the form of an unfair disadvantage. The coach of the team made several comparisons between the Powerade team and the other team to create an illusion of disadvantage, but the apparent advantages held by the opposing team did not create the illusion of genuine unfairness. The disabled person who triumphs over adversity, the small guy bullied in the playground, or the obese guy laughed at because he was dancing all create strong feelings of unfairness that leads to empathy towards the underdog. The Powerade commercial failed to create this degree of empathy, and therefore there were no resulting feelings of unfairness.

The third reason for failure was the absence of effort. The Powerade commercial doesn't include any evidence of effort, only several 'reminders' by the coach of the team's abilities. There needs to be clear evidence of effort – ability should be downplayed when it comes to creating an underdog theme. This final shortcoming prevented the Powerade advertisement from going viral.

Let's compare the Powerade advertisement to a delightful ad about some young girls doing something remarkable. GoldieBlox were new entrants into the fiercely competitive toy market dominated by Hasbro and Mattel. To break into the market they produced an ingenious viral advertisement using the theme: 'Little girls are underdogs, and our brand is here to help them triumph by using our toys'. Their 'Princess machine' (**https://youtu.be/IIGyVa5Xftw**) video advertisement currently has over 2.5 million views on YouTube.

The theme of the advertisement is of young girls claiming their place in a male-dominated world. The ad sets the scene with the unfair revelation that girls begin to lose confidence in maths and science by around age seven. The young girls, when faced with boredom watching TV, decide to demonstrate their analytical and engineering potential by constructing an elaborate Rube Goldberg machine using only their girly toys – demonstrating effort over ability. Most people's perceptions of young girls are as cute and vulnerable little people. But in the advertisement the girls are intelligent, powerful and capable human beings, triumphing over adversity by performing an impressive and surprising feat.

The advertisement is successful in creating an underdog theme because it meets the conditions of successful underdog positioning discussed earlier. First, there is an obvious separation between the brand and the girls – there is no affiliation. Second, the advertisement is successful at creating an illusion of unfairness. It is highly believable that young girls are disadvantaged in male-dominated professions such as engineering, and most women would agree that women are disadvantaged in the workforce in general. Despite women making up 46 per cent of the workforce, four in ten businesses worldwide have no women in senior management, and women earn less than men in 99 per cent of all occupations.

Finally, the 'Princess machine' viral ad shows clear evidence of effort over ability with the complexity of the Rube Goldberg machine. As I recommended earlier, ability should be downplayed at the expense of effort.

In contrast to the successful 'Princess machine' ad, the Powerade advertisement displays no evidence of effort since none of the players actually play, and so it's difficult to believe the team are deserving.

Changing people's beliefs

One of the most powerful forces in society is a sense of justice. You only have to read the comments on a Facebook news page to see how passionate people can get when it comes to someone or some group being treated unfairly. Justice is the foundation of a successful underdog story, but it can be even more powerful when the justice component is amplified.

One of my favourite viral ads of all time is one released in 2014. It's my favourite not because of its creativity, but rather because it's technically very strong, and ticks most of the boxes for my recommendations in this book! It's a great example of how to ramp up the justice component to activate a strong emotional response in the audience.

The aim of any viral should be to make people feel something. But the best of the best can change people's beliefs. The movie is Under Armour's 'I will what I want' (**https://youtu.be/H-V7cOestUs**), starring supermodel Gisele Bündchen. The movie begins with Gisele wearing Under Armour sportswear and facing a punching bag. The room is grey concrete, like a prison gymnasium, with only a sliver of sunlight crossing the room. Her fists are taped up, and she's not wearing any makeup. It's clear she means business.

The beginning of the video ad creates an interesting paradox because people usually associate supermodels with lean bodies and fashion gowns, not the hardness of a fight training room. This creates intrigue and curiosity that hook the viewer in.

Suddenly, Gisele begins to kick the punching bag. The surprising thing is that the kicks have the force and skill of a powerful and quick K1 boxer – far removed from the expectations of a glamourous supermodel.

Every day, thousands of people voice their opinion about Gisele on social media. Like many celebrities, she contends with many supporters, but also many critics. Social media comments about Gisele begin flashing on the walls of the basement. 'Gisele is just a model', 'Under Amour! WTF!?', 'Is modelling now a sport?', 'Stick to modelling sweetie', 'She's nothing special at all', 'Gisele is so fake', 'She's old', 'Model's only look good retouched'. Gisele then does something even more surprising. She moves into full combat mode, releasing a truly impressive assault on the punching bag, including a rapid series of powerful jabs. She steps back from the bag, and more comments begin to display on the wall. The catch phrase 'I will what I want' displays on screen. Gisele has just shown her critics something to make them feel embarrassed. The movie shows her determination and ability to fight for success. Clearly she puts in a lot of effort into her success, and this is demonstrated in a powerful metaphor with the fighting.

Gisele finds justice against those people who posted hurtful remarks about her in the best way possible, highlighting the injustice of social media trolling by showing the world that there is more to her than meets the eye, and that her success is deserved.

Comedians like Chris Rock have long known that people are strangely attracted to the unfairly disadvantaged. It can make people laugh, or it can melt their hearts. People are naturally drawn to support the underdog, and derive great satisfaction when they see an underdog win. For brands, positioning themselves as an underdog is a shortcut to rapid success, but it's not so easy to activate the sense of fairness and justice necessary to get people sharing. Creating an illusion of unfair disadvantage, where effort outshines ability, is the key to creating a successful underdog campaign. A true underdog has nothing to lose, but everything to gain.

Action plan for justice

A sense of justice is a powerful feeling that creates intrigue and motivates people to share. To create this sense of justice in your video advertisements, three conditions are necessary:

1 **Distance.** When creating an underdog theme you must ensure there is a distance between the disadvantaged person and the observer. The easiest way to ensure this distance is to use an underdog figure that is unknown. Ideally you need a completely independent and unknown entity. If using a fictional underdog character, ensure the character isn't a sponsored representation of your brand.

2 **Unfair disadvantage.** It is essential to create an unfair disadvantage, not just any disadvantage. An unfair disadvantage creates a sense of injustice, whereas a simple disadvantage will tend to be ignored. People will not feel empathy towards someone that is simply disadvantaged in some way. Creating a disadvantage without unfairness might even have the opposite effect of what is intended, and create a sense of schadenfreude, which is a human tendency to derive pleasure from the misfortunates of others, not the intended empathy and sense of injustice that you are aiming for. One way to paint a disadvantage as unfair is to humanise the disadvantaged character. People will not tend to feel empathy and develop a sense of injustice towards a homeless person on the street. But if the homeless person's name and story are known, it humanises them, and people are more likely to feel their circumstances are unfair.

3 **Effort not ability.** The third condition necessary for a successful underdog illusion is a clear emphasis on effort not ability. This means that the underdog character must appear to be trying to succeed, and the success is due to concerted effort, not because of superior skills. The aim is to create a sense of deservingness, and if there is no sense of effort, then deservingness cannot be created.

7

Herding

Like many people, on Friday nights I like to eat a take-away. There's a road very near to my house that has a variety of restaurants, and so I usually head down there. What's unique about this road is that there's a cluster of seven restaurants all next to each other that sell basically the same kind of cuisine – Malaysian Chinese. I love this style of Asian food, so I usually choose one of these restaurants. I have ordered from all of them over the years, and I can testify they all have authentic and delicious dishes. But there's something curious about these restaurants: one is always extremely busy while the other six are always quite empty. And it's not because of price, great restaurant reviews, or because it has more delicious food. The answer is more surprising.

The reason one of the restaurants is busier than the others is because it's the smallest. It has just four small tables inside, and for people ordering take-aways on a Friday night, there's no room to wait for their order inside, so everyone is forced to wait outside on the street. People who come down here to get their food see six empty restaurants, and one with a mass of people outside. They assume the restaurant with the people outside must have better tasting food, or some other unknown benefits, and line up outside as well. Even though it's logical to order from one of the empty restaurants instead.

When people are uncertain, and want to reduce the risk of making the wrong decision, they copy what others are doing. This is an example of 'herding'.

Following the crowd is an interesting feature of human behaviour. When we're in a group that's laughing, we'll tend to start laughing ourselves, or if we're in an audience that starts to clap, we'll join in and clap as well. On many occasions it's difficult not to be influenced by the crowd.

On social media and the internet in general, herding behaviour can be enormously beneficial for brands. A study conducted by Michael Luca at Harvard Business School found that a one star increase on review sites results in around a 5–9 per cent increase in revenue (Luca, 2011). People reduce their uncertainty of purchase by looking to others for clues on their likely experience.

On the face of it herding behaviour may seem quite trivial, but it can also be tragically destructive. Stampedes at large public gatherings are a form of herding that begins with people observing other people panicking and running that can lead to crushing injuries and death. Herding is also responsible for dozens of drownings each year from people swimming in unpatrolled and dangerous areas 'because other people were swimming there'.

Herding can also be very destructive and difficult to stop if the message spread is negative. A study conducted by Luis Cabral and colleagues at NYU Stern found that just one piece of negative feedback results in around a 13 per cent decrease in sales, and that future negative ratings are 25 per cent more likely to occur after people see that someone is already dissatisfied (Cabral and Hortaçsu, 2010). These statistics are a sober reminder to brands that the promise of social media is a double-edged sword – get it right and the benefits can be great; get it wrong and the consequences can be severe.

Jim's muesli mystery and the power of scarcity

Jim was a health nut, from a very early age. This made Jim unusual, since most of the kids at Jim's school preferred fast-food and fizzy drinks over vegetables and fruit. Unfortunately for Jim, his parents weren't into healthy eating, and so he had to learn how to make healthy food on his own. As a result, he got very good at making one food in particular – muesli. Over the years Jim recorded his unique muesli recipes in a ragged volume entitled 'Jim's exotic and delicious muesli recipes'. They included macadamia manuka pomegranate, Inca berry coconut, and chilli chocolate yogurt berry, among others.

Soon after graduating from high school, Jim got his first job as a short-order cook serving the breakfast shift at a local diner. Of course he detested serving the kind of food he despised, and eventually persuaded his boss to include a selection of his unique muesli recipes on the menu. His initiative paid off – it turned out there were other people in his town who also wanted to eat more healthily. And slowly the diner developed a reputation for serving the most delicious and healthiest breakfast in town. He eventually caught the attention of the head chef at the most prestigious restaurant in town – the main dining room at the Amethyst Hotel. The chef invited Jim to train as an apprentice. Jim learned how to refine his cooking skills, and over the years eventually worked his way up to become the hotel's executive chef.

As any executive chef will tell you, one of the challenges for any restaurant is finding a careful balance between ordering enough food so the restaurant doesn't run out, and making sure the food is as fresh as possible. Jim became quite skilled at ordering the right amount of ingredients for most dishes, except for his collection of breakfast muesli. He usually had five different recipes of his muesli available on the breakfast buffet on any given day, and at the end of each month he dropped the least popular flavour, and introduced a new one from his infamous muesli recipe book. The problem was that he couldn't properly estimate how much of any one flavour would be consumed in a month, and therefore couldn't estimate the quantity of ingredients he needed to order for each recipe. An unpopular flavour one month would be the most popular the following month, or the most popular flavour would become the least popular.

Jim was baffled and had to find out what was going on. He first questioned his sous chefs thinking they were perhaps altering his recipes between each batch. The chefs testified that they always followed the recipes to the letter. He then questioned the hotel staff to see if there were differences in the types of people that were staying in the hotel each month. Again his investigation drew a blank. Finally, Jim decided the only way he could get to the bottom of the mystery was to observe people choosing his muesli during breakfast service.

Breakfast service began at 6 am each morning. Jim arrived early to help the buffet manager set up. Each cereal was presented in a large glass serving jar, with a metal scoop, and a cardboard placard with details of the flavour and ingredients. The buffet manager explained to Jim that when a new cereal was introduced on the first day of each month, he moved all the jars over to the left, and put the new cereal on the right.

As the customers drifted in and out, Jim observed his coveted muesli collection with a watchful eye. He observed that the new cereal located on the right was the most popular with the diners. This fit his inventory observations – the new muesli recipe for the month was always the most popular. By the time the breakfast session was over, the new cereal flavour jar was almost empty. Curiously, the other cereals had hardly been touched, despite at least one of them being hugely popular the previous month.

Jim wondered if the customers preferred the new cereal flavour simply because it was new. But that couldn't be right because the guests weren't likely staying in the hotel the previous month. There was also nothing on the placard or anywhere around the muesli to suggest it was the new flavour.

Jim was at a loss.

Disappointed that he had not solved the mystery, Jim decided to return the following month to see if he could notice any changes. He arrived early again to help the buffet manager set things up. As he was placing the jars of muesli next to each other on the buffet, he noticed something that he hadn't noticed the last time. He noticed that the amounts of muesli in each jar were uneven. Specifically, the new muesli just introduced for the month had less in the jar than the others, and the popular muesli from the previous month had more in the jar than the others.

Maybe nothing he thought, but he had a hunch. Was it possible that the amount of muesli in each jar affected how popular the muesli was? He decided to play a little experiment. He took all the jars into the back kitchen, and scooped out muesli from each jar until they were all perfectly even. He then took extra scoops of muesli out of one of the jars, so that it had less than the others. He ended up with five jars that had the exact same amount of muesli, and one jar with less.

As the patrons started to arrive, he took his corner to keep a watchful eye on his muesli. Soon into the service, he began to witness something quite remarkable. Almost all of the diners were choosing the jar with the least muesli inside, even though it wasn't the new flavour of the month, or even the most popular flavour from the previous month. Jim was intrigued.

Without realising it, Jim was witnessing a psychological response to scarcity. Jim's muesli flavours were all unique and exotic. Flavours like macadamia manuka pomegranate, Inca berry coconut, and chilli chocolate yogurt berry might have sounded interesting and perhaps delicious, but without having tried any of the flavours before, likely the diners would have been very uncertain about which one to choose. The decision would have also been risky since the diners wouldn't have had previous experience with the muesli, and no one wants to choose a flavour they'll later regret. When people are faced with a decision under uncertainty, they'll tend to look for clues to help them decide. The most obvious clue would have been that one of jars had less muesli in it than the other jars. The diners would have assumed that other people knew something about this flavour of muesli that they didn't know. Likely, they would have reached the conclusion that because that jar had less, then it must have been the most delicious. This would have started a snowball effect – the more muesli consumed, the more popular it would have become.

So why was Jim observing the new muesli being the most popular when it was first released, then becoming the least popular the following month?

The sous chefs would only make a limited amount of a new muesli flavour to avoid wastage. The buffet manager, knowing that the new flavour always ran out quickly, only filled the jar up halfway to ensure it wouldn't run out before the end of the month. What he didn't realise was that by filling the jar up halfway he was actually speeding up consumption. The following month the sous chefs would make double the amount, thinking that it would continue to be popular. The buffet manager would then fill the jar to the brim, not realising that doing so effectively killed the popularity. As a result, the new muesli was popular when it was first released and unpopular the following month. The sharp drop in consumption led to waste, which explained Jim's problem ordering the right amount of raw ingredients.

Underlying the success of many viral campaigns is herding behaviour – people following what others are doing. Scarcity is a form of herding behaviour – when people are uncertain about what to do, they'll assume others have information they don't have, and will copy.

How Ray Kroc got people to eat burgers

In 1955, Ray Kroc put up a sign outside his McDonald's franchise in Des Plains, Illinois, claiming to have sold over one million hamburgers. He noticed a spike in sales, and so decided to put the same sign on all McDonald's franchises. Within 12 months of Ray Kroc putting up his first

Figure 7.1   Source: © 123rf.com

sign, McDonald's had sold five million hamburgers, and after eight years it had sold one billion.

By 1994, McDonald's executives announced that they would stop counting the number of hamburgers, since the total number was estimated to be over 99 billion. The power of the hamburger count had run its course, and by then McDonald's was the largest hamburger restaurant in the world, serving 68 million customers daily across 119 countries. Ray Kroc, a paper cup salesman from Chicago, had built an empire.

Herding occurs when people copy the crowd because they're uncertain. 'Social proof' is evidence that a significant number of people have behaved in a certain way. A website might have a list of current customers, testimonials, and statistics on how many people have previously purchased. This social proof might influence new visitors to also purchase.

Social proof

To reduce uncertainty, people will copy the crowd. Social proof is evidence of crowd behaviour.

Social proof can be used in creative ways. Brazilian apparel retailer C&A embeds digital counters in their clothes hangers showing the number of Facebook 'Likes' on their page. Hotel.com displays the number of people who have booked a particular hotel room in the past few hours. Naked Wines displays how many people would buy different wines again. Each of these examples uses social proof to reduce customer uncertainty and increase decisions to purchase.

Whether it's a small Malaysian Chinese restaurant, or the largest restaurant chain in the world, people will reduce their uncertainty of purchase by looking at what others have done. Herding is a powerful force behind decision making and the spread of information.

Seeding

In March 2012, the Invisible Children charity released a short film to raise awareness about an African militia leader named Joseph Kony who was forcefully recruiting children soldiers in the Ugandan Sudanese area to commit brutal crimes. The movie earned 43 million views in just two days.

One of the mechanisms contributing to the incredibly rapid spread of the Kony movie was celebrity endorsement. Oprah Winfrey is credited with initiating the celebrity endorsement under the hashtag #Kony2012 on her Twitter account. The campaign recruited 20 celebrities to share and endorse the movie, including George Clooney, Angelina Jolie and Oprah, and 12 'policy makers' including George Bush, Condoleezza Rice and John Kerry.

The Kony movie illustrates something important about the spread of viral content. The rapid spread of the Kony movie was caused by people acting on celebrity authority and respect, but it also illustrates how people are connected, and how social structure facilitates the spread of information. For a viral to be successful, it needs to be 'seeded', which is the placement of shareable content in a way that's accessible to predefined groups of people. Some people are able to spread information to more people than others. And some networks and groups facilitate the spread easier than others. Seeding determines how successful the content is towards becoming viral.

Seeding

The exposure and placement of new content to maximise person-to-person spread.

People are organised into networks. A network is essentially a group of people who are bound by some common interest or cause. Most of us belong to at least one network, though many people belong to several, including family networks, work colleagues, clubs or Church groups. Sometimes the networks we belong to are volitional, meaning we have control over our membership like our circle of friends. Sometimes they're not volitional, like the network of people we work with. One thing all networks facilitate is communication among its members. If we're a member of a network, we communicate with others in that network.

Networks are important when seeding shareable content because they provide the catalyst for sharing. The success of shareable content often depends on how it is seeded. If the shareable content is released into a small network with few connections, or to the wrong people within a network, then success is significantly lowered. Choosing the correct network to seed is important because for something to go viral it needs to spread quickly. If the rate of spread is too slow, the spread will stall too early, and the network effect will be lost. The faster a viral spreads in the early stages, the more likely the content will survive.

Influencers

People who are taken notice of and who tend to have many followers.

Many have credited the rapid spread and ultimate success of Facebook to the way it was diffused into the Harvard student body, and subsequently leaked into other universities. As soon as one university was saturated, it spilled over to neighbouring universities. Interestingly, it was the Ivy League universities that adopted Facebook first, suggesting that income and education status were two of the factors influencing Facebook's spread.

When computer simulation programs are used to model networks, the graphical representation kind of looks like bicycle wheels. Each has a central hub, with spokes that represent connections between people. The reason why networks tend to have a central hub is because there are usually one or more people in a network who have proportionately more connections than everyone else. They might be a leader, or an organiser, or someone that's simply very popular. People who are hubs are called 'influencers'. They are typically well connected people, and have influence over others in some way.

Figure 7.2   Source: © Ian Dagnall/ Alamy Stock Photo

People tend to value what influencers say, and influencers tend to have many followers. Of course there will be spokes criss-crossing and connecting people within the network who are not influencers as well.

The other key feature of networks when represented graphically is the 'spokes' that appear to join one wheel with another wheel. These are people who have connections in more than one network. For example, someone might be a member of a Church group, and also be a member of a car club. These people are called 'bridges' and they connect one network to another.

Why is knowing this important? Quite simply, influencers determine how fast your viral spreads, and bridges determine how far it will spread. The secret to successfully seeding a viral is knowing how to get these two types of people to share.

Bridges

People who have membership across groups.

Sometimes it's easy to find an influencer – someone who is CEO of a company or captain of a team for example. Other times the influencers are less obvious to find. Frequently they have a large audience, such as bloggers, celebrities or journalists. Tools like Klout can be used to find these people since influencers typically have many connections on social media. Once an influencer is found, the task is to get them to endorse or share your intended viral content. This could be done through incentives, or by simply working towards building a solid relationship with them.

The best chance to influence a bridge to share to a new network is to flood the existing network as much as possible, since almost all networks contain many more bridges than they do influencers. The hope is that a bridge in a network will also be an influencer in another network, to drive inter-network spread. This is not always the case however, and it's often not the most influential person who has the biggest impact on viral spread, but rather it is the most easily influenced person.

Anti-herders (and what makes cool cool?)

When content gains viral momentum and other people see how popular it is, the herding instinct kicks in which adds more fuel to the fire of spread. But it's a chicken and egg situation. You need social proof for a viral to kick off, but social proof needs lots of people already sharing the content.

Herding behaviour works both ways – if people see other people sharing they'll be more likely to share, but if they don't see other people sharing, it acts as a disincentive.

One solution to this problem is to focus on seeding to people in a network who are über-influencers – people who are admired and impact the behaviours and attitudes of others. These people don't follow the herd, they lead the herd. They are 'anti-herders'.

Anti-herders take pride in not following the crowd, and in fact will often go out of their way to be different. Everett Rogers, who developed a theory to explain the diffusion of innovations theory, identified a class of people he termed 'innovators'. These are the first to try new technologies, and influence the adoption of technologies by others (Rogers, 2003). Anti-herders are also trendsetters, and leaders in the culture and fashion of youth.

Innovators

Venturesome people who are the first to try new things.

Anti-herders are people who are usually the first to adopt new things, and take pride in being one of the first. They want to be seen by their peers as on top of things, and in the know with current styles and trends. They are the trendsetters, not the trend-followers. These are the people who trawl charity shops looking for rare clothes, or drive cars that are rare or unique, or visit countries that no one else would dream of visiting. Because they go out of their way to be different, they're motivated to find things of value before anyone else. They're like goldminers – value for them is rarity and uniqueness, and they will work very hard to find it.

Because of their uniqueness, people are intrigued by anti-herders and will tend to look up to them. They are often considered experts in the latest styles and trends, and people respect their efforts to step out of the norm and stick it to the man. Recall the Sex Pistols in the 1970s. They were anti-everything, but ironically they shaped the trends of youth culture that still echo to this day.

Anti-herder

Someone who doesn't follow the crowd, and takes pride in being different.

Anti-herders are powerful for two reasons. First, they're likely to share something that's cool if they know they're one of the first (your viral is cool right?). Second, they usually have a lot of reference power in their networks, and persuade others easily.

The main trick to capturing the interests of anti-herders is signalling scarcity. Anti-herders are goldminers. Value for them is stuff that's rare. Although everyone places value on scarcity, anti-herders are affected by scarcity more than herding behaviour.

One recent trend that uses scarcity and the attraction of anti-herders to help spread in the early stages is the practice of 'pre-launching'. This is a common strategy with new businesses that are about to launch. The idea is to create buzz surrounding the impending release of the app, by creating an exclusive member's only preview. If the promise is cool enough, anti-herders jump on board relishing the idea of being the first.

Photo sharing app Hipster is a great example. To create hype around its launch, the start-up spread the word around San Francisco that something very cool was coming to the Bay area. This piqued people's interest, and it wasn't long before bloggers and media folk started to speculate what might be about to happen. The Hipster website consisted of just one simple page with a form where people could leave their email address to get put on the invite list. If signees invited three of their friends, then they earned earlier access to the service than everyone else. The website attracted 10,000 signups in just two days.

Another example was the life-timeline app Lifepath. The service began as invite only, inviting people to purchase an 'entrance ticket' before the app was even launched. The scarcity created the illusion that this was something everyone must have, and resulted in thousands of signups. The closer to the release date, the cheaper the entrance tickets became. On a side note, interestingly, there were more registrations sold when the price was $10 than when the price was just $3. This is actually an artefact of something else called the price–quality heuristic. Essentially people associate the quality of something based on its price – the more expensive something is, the higher the quality people believe it to be. When people thought the quality was higher, based on the higher price, they were more likely to sign up.

Anti-herders are the key to kick starting a viral in its early stages, since they're affected by valuable but scarce things, and make a conscious effort to not be affected by herding behaviour. Anti-herders are influential, and will help spread the viral in its early stages, motivated to share the viral when still relatively unknown. Once the viral starts to gather momentum and become known, social proof helps the viral to spread, as more people start to share the viral.

Your opinions are not your own

In late April 2015, one story dominated the headlines more than any other. Two Australian drug smugglers were about to be executed in Indonesia for attempting to smuggle 18 pounds of heroin from Indonesia into Australia. The method of death was firing squad, to be carried out on a remote beach in the early hours of the morning. Appeal after appeal had failed. Politicians and even rock stars made personal appeals to the President of Indonesia to spare the men's lives, but to no avail. At 3.25 am on the morning of 29 April 2015 shots echoing across the bay signalled their fate. Andrew Chan and Myuran Sukumaran were executed with three bullets each to the heart.

Media coverage in the days leading up to the executions spanned the globe. Each story released sparked passionate debate through social media. People generally took one of two sides – either they were compassionate and wished the men could be spared. Or, they took the position that perhaps the men deserved their fate since smuggling drugs was a hideous crime and the men knew the risks.

What was interesting was the way people were split in their decisions. There were a limited number of facts on the case, and most news stories simply recycled the same facts from the news wires. Some of the news stories were dominated by reader comments suggesting they deserved the execution. Other news stories were dominated by comments suggesting the men should be spared. But there were no news stories where the opinions were evenly mixed. Despite the news stories all reporting similar facts, there was a significant difference in opinion for each story.

Groupthink

A phenomenon where someone forms an opinion based on the collective opinion of the group, not their individual beliefs.

What was the cause of such diverse polarisation? The reason is a phenomenon whereby people form attitudes and opinions based on the crowd, and this is known as 'groupthink'.

Groupthink occurs when a group of people reach a collective consensus on an idea, despite individual differences in opinion. People who disagree with the collective decision or opinion tend to keep quiet because they don't want to disrupt the harmony of the group. Worse, they don't want the group to resent them for having an opinion that no one else shares. As a result, by habit people will adopt the prevailing opinion in a group.

The goal of many group gatherings is often to reach a consensus, and so the temptation by everyone is to forego personal opinions in an effort to just go with the crowd, even if several other members also share the different opinion. The danger is that the wrong decision is reached.

There will always be people who will argue against the group, but by and large people will tend to adopt the opinion of the majority. This has led companies and whole nations to folly when the collective decisions have been misjudged and wrong. Many believe for example that the Space Shuttle Challenger disaster in 1986 was a result of groupthink. Engineers who knew of the dangers of launching in low temperatures followed the collective decision made by NASA managers to just go ahead. The shuttle exploded 73 seconds into its flight, killing everyone aboard.

Groupthink can help creative content go viral. If the majority think something is worthy, other people will also start to believe it is worthy. But groupthink can also be dangerous in viral campaigns. Just like the kid who is being bullied at school, it's almost impossible to become popular when you're already on the back foot. Once your viral stirs a negative response, it's almost impossible to turn it around, especially if the bully is an influencer.

Companies who try to capitalise on human suffering reported in the news often fall foul of any genuine intentions to help others. Whenever a viral campaign creates a moral dilemma, there is a high chance of groupthink forming.

Bing for example famously offered to give $1 to Japan earthquake victims, but with a catch. People had to retweet the Bing pledge through Twitter before the $1 was paid. This created a moral dilemma and rampant negative groupthink set in. People complained that Bing was using the natural disaster as a marketing opportunity, forcing Bing to abandon the campaign, make a $100k donation, and issue a public apology. The negative response was viral, and the damage to their brand was immeasurable.

Asking for 'Retweets' or 'Likes' in return for a natural disaster donation is surprisingly common, and serves to emphasise the dangers of creating a moral dilemma in advertising. Papa John's Pizza made an almost identical mistake as Bing, offering to donate $1 to starving children in return for a 'Like' or 'Share'. Korean carmaker Kia also promised to donate to World Vision in return for Facebook 'Likes'. Both companies suffered tremendous backlash from subscribers on social media accusing the companies of using natural disasters as a marketing opportunity.

Despite the best intentions, groupthink can be destructive of viral campaigns and marketers should be careful they don't create a moral dilemma that could trigger negative groupthink. Trying to become popular is almost impossible when you're being talked about in a negative way. All it takes is one influencer who takes exception to your capitalistic ways, and you're virally doomed.

When you think about our strong tendency to copy others, you start to question why we so readily hand over control of our behaviour. Most people would prefer to think that they are in control of their destiny, but often times we're not.

Herding is important for making a viral spread rapidly. If a viral doesn't gain momentum quickly, it stalls, and will die pretty quick.

It begins with uncertainty. When we're uncertain about what to do, we search for clues to help us decide the best course of action. If there are other people behaving in a certain way, we assume they know something we don't know, and we'll tend to follow their lead as a shortcut to gaining knowledge that we don't have.

Action plan for herding

Seeding is the strategy you choose to maximise the chances of sharing. It's important that you seed your content in appropriate networks to maximise the chances of viral success.

1   **Choose networks.** The first step is to identify a suitable network to seed your content. Three criteria should be kept in mind:

   (a)   the network chosen must be large (at least one thousand);

   (b)   members must be closely related to each other on psychographic and demographic variables; and

   (c)   the networks must be close to each other in terms of frequency and volume of everyday communication.

Psychographic variables include personality traits, values, attitudes, interests and lifestyle choices. Demographic variables include geographic proximity, age, income and education. The more closely related people are in the network, the faster your content will get shared. One example of a network of people who are closely related to each other on these three variables is university students. They are all approximately the same age, they are highly social with each other, and they share many interests. They also tend to have a larger than average circle of friends. When considering a viable network, relevancy of your content and brand (if applicable) to the network is also critically important.

2   **Choose the correct people.** The next step is to identify the correct people in the network. Ideally you want to identify anti-herders to begin with. Anti-herders will have larger than normal networks, greater influence, and might often be more social than normal members. Occasionally anti-herders hold leadership positions in a network, but not always. Tools such as Klout can be used to find people in the network with high influence. Once an anti-herder is identified, they can be incentivised to share your content. The incentive could be monetary or other. It is important to note that anti-herders by definition will be reluctant to be seen as following the crowd, so it is important they are identified and approached early, before your content starts to spread.

3   **Highlight social proof.** After your content begins to spread, herding effects will boost sharing. When your content starts to spread, it creates a herding effect, where the rate of spread gains momentum as more people share. Social proof is the evidence that creates the herding effect. Vanity metrics such as the number of 'Shares', 'Likes' or 'Retweets' are the most salient form of social proof. The number of views on YouTube for example will increase exponentially as the view count grows past a certain value (tens of thousands). Another powerful form of social proof is media coverage. If your content is interesting enough, or is showing signs of going viral, it might attract attention from the media. Any media coverage further boosts the viral sharing. Key people in the media should be followed on Twitter and notified about any content that appears to be getting traction.

8 CHAPTER EIGHT
Groups

In early 2015, Cecilia Bleasdale emailed a photo of a dress to her daughter Grace who was about to get married. She was planning to wear the dress to the wedding, and wanted to know what Grace thought.

When Grace opened the email and looked at the photo she was surprised. She had instructed everybody to wear dark-coloured dresses to the wedding, but the picture of the dress her mother sent was white and gold. This would not do she thought to herself. Grace called her fiancé Kier over to have a look. He glanced at the photo, and grimaced at his wife to be. 'Nice joke darling. That blue and black dress will look fantastic on your Mum!' Grace scorned back at him. 'What are you talking about; it's obviously white and gold!'

And so the argument began.

The singer at Grace's wedding was intrigued that people saw the dress as different colours, and on the Monday after the wedding decided to post the image on her Tumblr page. By Thursday the page was getting an incredible 140,000 views per minute. Within a week the page had a total of 73 million views, and 483,000 comments. Half of the internet thought the dress was white and gold, and the other half thought it was blue and black.

The world had gone berserk over the colour of a dress!

The dress

I'm sure you've been in a situation when you were certain you were right and the other person was wrong. Likely the other person felt they were right, and you were wrong, and you argued as a result. One of you is wrong – but neither of you are willing to concede. So why is it you're both willing to defend your position?

Kristin Laurin and her colleagues at Stanford University set out to find the answer to this mystery (Laurin, *et al.*, 2013). In a series of experiments they found that people are motivated to 'rationalise' situations that are likely to persist, and one way people rationalise their situation is by consoling themselves and arguing with others that their situation is correct. For example, a person in a bad relationship will argue with others that their relationship is fine, even though to an outsider it seems crazy that the couple are still together, because they've come to a realisation that their situation can't be easily changed. When someone believes that their situation is unchangeable, they'll rationalise their situation to make it more bearable. 'Oh but it'll be worse if I change' or 'Things will get better' are commonly heard objections. As a result of rationalisation, people convince themselves that they're right, and others are wrong.

Rationalisation

The tendency of people to justify their behaviour or thoughts to avoid a self-realisation that their situation is intolerable and not admirable.

Rationalisation is one of the mechanisms contributing to the dress argument. When someone sees a white and gold dress, they find it difficult to accept that other people see it as blue and black. Because they can't change what they see, this leads them to rationalise their beliefs. Strangely, people felt compelled to defend the colours that they saw. In the initial stages of the dress argument, there was passionate debate between the two groups – those who saw blue and black and those who saw white and gold. During this debate, people were motivated to seek support from others they knew. On everyone's mind was 'I wonder what colour my friend/girlfriend/boyfriend sees?' This created buzz on social media as the phenomenon began to spread. It was this buzz that kick-started the sharing. By the time scientists began to weigh in with theories for why people saw different colours the spread had changed from an argument of interest to a global news story.

Join the club

Spanish beer brand Mahou-San Miguel wanted to raise awareness of their brand. Their target market is males between the ages of 18 to 50, and an upcoming football match in Madrid between Atlético Madrid and Real Madrid provided the perfect opportunity.

They developed a phone app that consisted of a street map of the city, and a quiz. The questions in the quiz were about the beloved game of football. For each quiz question answered correctly, the user earned points that were counted towards their team. The app used geolocation to determine where people were answering the quiz questions from. Any user of the app could 'win' the street they were in by answering the quiz question correctly. When a street had been won, it would change into the team's colour on the map. The only way the opposing team could change the colour back to their own team colours was by answering more of the quiz questions correctly than the opposition. Although the campaign only ran for two weeks, Madrid's neighbourhoods were conquered and re-conquered more than 80,000 times. The campaign was enormously successful, earning more than 36 million media mentions.

The app was very successful at sorting the city of Madrid into groups based on loyalties to a football club. The brilliance of the app was that users got a real sense of being part of the team and battling against the opposition. Each team could conquer parts of the city which gave the user real-time feedback on their team strength, and provided a strong incentive for users to continue to use the app.

I'm sure you've belonged to a sports team, club or Church group at some point in your life. It's interesting to think about why people feel the need to join groups. Early in human history, belonging to a group served a survival function. It was easier to hunt for food and defend against threats when in a group. Children also stood a better chance of survival when attached to a group, ensuring lineage of the gene pool.

The success of the Mahou-San Miguel campaign illustrates how people are willing to defend the beliefs of their group. When someone is a member of a group, they have a tendency to defend what binds the group together and what defines their reason for membership. For the participants of the Mahou-San Miguel campaign, it was the love of their football club that bonded them together. The app created a way for the members to defend their reason for membership – their shared love for their team. This was the brilliance behind the Mahou-San Miguel campaign – the app provided an all-inclusive platform for all members of each group to defend their territory. The tendencies to participate would have been primeval and instinctive.

In the Mahou-San Miguel campaign, membership in either team may be thought of as voluntary, since people have a choice over who they would prefer to support. But in 'the dress' groups, membership is involuntary since people don't really have a choice over which colour they see. When the reason for membership is involuntary, people will rationalise their membership. The motives to defend their membership are a product of this rationalisation, whereby people have convinced themselves of their loyalty because their membership to an opposing team cannot be changed.

What Mahou-San Miguel and the dress have in common, aside from both going viral, is that they manage to side people into one of two groups, and motivate each group to defend the tie that binds the group together. With the dress it was the colour of the dress that people were compelled to defend. With Mahou-San Miguel it was the sports team. When members of a group are motivated to defend the common tie that binds the group together, they'll tend to call on others to support them. The group binds together in unity causing buzz as communications fly, and members seek reinforcements. With group-based virals, it's this buzz that drives the initial spread.

Like a girl

In 2014 Procter & Gamble released the superviral 'Always #LikeAGirl'. To date the video has two million shares. The video puts into question the observation that someone might do something 'like a girl'. The video suggests that the term 'like a girl' is not only derogatory, but also damaging to girls' self-confidence.

The ad begins by showing a theatre stage, and a group of production staff sitting in the seating section. One-by-one various male and female actors come onto the stage to audition. They're all in their late teens to early 20s.

Each actor is asked to 'run like a girl'. They all run on the spot in a goofy way, swaying their arms and flicking their heels out awkwardly. Then they're asked to 'fight like a girl'. The styles are comical, resembling various forms of cat scratching or slapping techniques. Finally they're asked to 'throw a ball like a girl'. Again, the actions are goofy and comical. None of them question what it means to behave like a girl. They simply interpret what they believe the judges want to see.

In the following scene, young children are invited onto the stage one-by-one and asked the same questions. Except this time when they're asked to run like a girl, the child actors sprint quickly on the spot. When they're asked to throw a ball they pretend to throw like a baseball player. When they're asked to fight like a girl they punch like a boxer. The children, both boys and girls, don't understand what it means to do something 'like a girl'.

The ad ends with explanations from the older girls on how hurtful and damaging to their self-esteem it is to be told that they do something 'like a girl'.

The 'Always #LikeAGirl' advertisement illustrates a 'fixed group difference', whereby someone is a member of a group because of a reason that's largely beyond their control or not easily changed. West coast/east coast, young/old, vegetarian/meat eater, are all fixed groups where members can't easily change their membership, or membership is not overtly voluntary. Fixed groups are in contrast to voluntary groups, such as sports teams or political parties, where membership is voluntary and more intentional, and can be changed more easily.

The way to spark debate between fixed groups, and therefore motivate sharing of information as group members seek support, is to question their reason for difference. Since membership can't be easily changed, members will rationalise their membership, and feel compelled to defend it. The women in the 'Always #LikeAGirl' advertisement are embarrassed or angered by the fact that they're perceived to do things differently. The concept of 'like a girl' puts their differences into question by creating a source of contentiousness, which drives sharing as members discuss the source of contention and seek support from others.

Fixed group difference

Two or more groups where membership is non-volitional and cannot be easily changed (e.g. male/female, young/old).

The dress phenomenon had a similar mechanism driving the viral spread. People saw either one colour or the other, though this was not by choice.

The reason for the group's differences was directly challenged because one group couldn't see what the other group were seeing. People felt compelled to share and comment on the dress because it was unbelievable that other people couldn't see what they could see.

Groups can be a powerful force towards unlocking the power of viral spread. Ancient instincts to defend membership of social groups can be extremely effective for marketers if they understand how to incorporate these desires into their campaign. When membership can't be easily changed, people rationalise their membership and are willing to defend it. This creates 'buzz' that helps spread the source of contention that drives word-of-mouth and contributes to the viral success of fixed group marketing campaigns.

Action plan for group-initiated viral share

People are social animals – most people have a desire to join groups. Membership can either be voluntary, or involuntary (fixed membership). In both cases, members of a group can be prompted to fight for their membership if their reason for membership is challenged. When the reason for membership is put into question, or the group is challenged, this motivates the group to bond together and fight. This creates sharing as group members seek support from each other, and seek to validate their membership.

Steps for initiating group-based viral share:

1 **Find a probable split in your target audience.** The first step towards creating successful group-based viral share is to identify separate and significantly sized groups in your target market. Each group must be significantly different from the other, and be large enough to create sufficient buzz. For some brands, finding a split might be relatively easy. A snow sports retailer might use a snowboarder/skier split. An education company might use a post-graduate/undergraduate split. But for many brands the membership might be less obvious and therefore more problematic. A viable option is to look for a fixed group difference. The obvious choice is gender, but other possibilities could include: lifestyle preference, geographical location, age or family status. There must be sufficient numbers in each group. Ensure the size of each group is big enough to ensure a meaningful comparison.

▶

2   **Define the ties that bind the group together and the group difference.** Before a campaign can be formulated, the ties that bind the group together must be identified. Usually, but not always, the ties are the same as the differentiating factor between the groups. Loyalists to a sports team are tied together because of their love for their team. The differentiating factor is their team. But consider the snowboarder/skier differentiation. The tie that binds snowboarders and skiers together in each of their respective groups is the same – both love sliding down snow-covered mountains. The difference between the groups is related to culture. Snowboarder culture is arguably characterised by a skater type rebelliousness. Skier culture is more reserved, like cycling. In this example, the cultural difference between the groups is more pronounced than the tie that binds each one together. It is important that the ties or differences defined in each group are important to group members. Skiers and snowboarders might have different tastes in fashion, but is that really important to them that they would fight for their style of apparel?

3   **Formulate a source of contentiousness.** Once the tie that binds the group together or group difference is identified, then the process can begin to challenge the difference. For an educational company segmenting at the level of tertiary education, the tie that binds the post-graduate group together could be life experience. Undergraduates might be tied together through the social experience that comes with early adulthood. A source of contention that could cause each group to rationalise and fight for their membership status could be wisdom. Post-graduates are likely to hold dear the fact that they have more experience in life and are therefore wiser. Undergraduates are likely to hold dear their new-found freedom as adults, and probably resent being treated as naive or juvenile. The source of contention could be evoked by a competition such as: 'Who really is the wisest when it comes to the art of living life?' It is important that the source of contention is shared between each group. Having one group care about a source of contention while another group is indifferent will not lead to a passionate debate.

4   **Implement a mechanism whereby members of each group can join in the fight.** The Mahou-San Miguel campaign successfully used a

105

mobile app to ensure all members of each group could contribute. Social media also provides the basic tools if the source of contention can be communicated in a shareable image or movie.

You should be cautious if using fixed group difference not to cause offence. Some group divisions are considered dangerous ground, including racial or socio-economic status, and if chosen should be treated with care.

Basing your campaign on a reasonable injustice of one group against another might be OK, but basing your campaign on a difference that might not be perceived by one group as a fair injustice might not be OK. The passion to defend one's group might turn into a backlash if the group perceives your brand to be 'stirring the pot' for the sake of getting a reaction. Obviously divisions based on ethnicity or religion are likely to be in poor taste and should be avoided.

9

CHAPTER NINE
Bump

The first video advertisement to reach one million views on YouTube was a Nike ad (**https://youtu.be/KNwLn85I75Y**). The advertisement went viral in October 2005, eight months after YouTube was founded.

The advertisement featured footage of the Brazilian footballer Ronaldinho receiving a new pair of Nike football boots. He puts the new boots on while sitting down on the grass, then stands up and proceeds to play with a ball. He juggles the ball with his feet, balances it on his head, and kicks it at a goal crossbar. The most impressive part is that he's able to kick the ball and bounce it off the top bar of the goal from 100 metres away, and then regain control of it before it touches the ground. He does this several times.

At the time the advertisement was considered revolutionary. The concept of the ad has been replicated many times since, including on several occasions by Nike again, though using different sports stars.

What's wrong with video advertising?

Before the internet, TV advertisers had it easy. There were a limited number of TV channels, almost everyone watched TV, and it was impossible to fast-forward or skip advertisements. Until the mid-1980s most people didn't even have remote controls so were forced to endure ads, unless of course they felt energetic enough to get off the couch. Marketers had everyone's attention, whether they liked it or not.

But the game has changed. Nowadays people can escape advertising with relative ease. Ad blockers, fastforwarding, and close buttons are just some of the ways consumers escape advertising.

The Nike 'Ronaldinho' advertisement did more than just break the magical one million views mark. It also redefined the basic structure of digital video advertising. Up until 2005 when the Nike 'Ronaldinho' ad came out, advertisers were still thinking about internet video advertising in the same way as TV advertising. Almost all internet video advertisements were using the same style as TV ads since there were no templates for internet video advertising and few examples of advertising that had gone viral.

TV-style advertising comes in a variety of styles. There's the so-called 'realist' style that shows a real-life situation that the target audience can relate to. Shampoo advertisements often follow this style: the girl has frizzy hair, she washes her hair with the product, her hair becomes magically smooth and glossy and she's smiling with joy. Then there's the 'documentary' style that includes interviews of people who work for the brand; or the 'talking heads' style that's a series of interviews of users of the brand; or the 'series' style which is more like a drama that's played out through several ads over time.

Around the time of the Nike 'Ronaldinho' advertisement, marketers began to realise a few things. First, TV-style advertising on the internet doesn't work well. Second, internet users can easily escape advertising on the internet. Third, and most important, on the internet ads can go viral.

Most marketers want to create an ad that people genuinely want to watch, but obviously there is difficulty. Most of it comes down to relevancy, and making sure the right people see the ad. If I'm looking to book a holiday in Japan, I'd welcome ads that notify me of sale fares to Japan. But showing people ads who don't want to see them can not only annoy, it can also damage perceptions of the brand. In effect, if their advertisements aren't welcome, then some brands are paying to be disliked rather than liked.

The structure of bump

Video ad campaigns on the internet have come a long way since the early days of internet advertising. Through trial and error and estimations of what causes an ad to go viral, marketers have identified a unique style of video ad suited to the internet – a style that has the right structure to maximise the chances of capturing people's attention and being shared. It's called 'Branded Viral Movie Production' (BVMP – pronounced 'bump').

Bump's guiding principle is that advertising is an exchange in value between the advertiser and the consumer: 'In exchange for your valuable time taken to watch my ad, I'll show you something that will affect you in a positive way'. This is a different mindset to the traditional 'I'm going to be as noisy/different as possible to catch your attention'. People don't want noise, and that's certainly not giving people a reason to share. Bump is designed to maximise sharing and minimise annoyance.

Branded Viral Movie Production (BVMP)

A video that has been designed to go viral on the internet.

One of the main features of bump is a 'transformative' structure. Transformational type advertising 'transforms' the viewer to imagine the experience, feelings and emotions of using the brand. This is in contrast to informational type advertising where the focus is on the features of the product. The Nike 'Ronaldinho' ad, for example, forces the viewer to wonder what it must be like to wear the football boots and have the skills necessary to perform amazing tricks wearing the boots. There is no specific information on what the boots are made of or any technology or comfort facts as there would be in a traditional informational type advertisement. Although transformational advertising did exist prior to the internet, it's important to note that the vast majority of ads that go viral online have a transformational style. Only people who are in the market to buy are attracted to product design facts as found in traditional informational type advertising. (Though of course there are always exceptions, such as the Blendtec 'Will it Blend?' series where founder Tom Dickson puts unusual things like iphones and golf balls into his blender to see what will happen.) By and large most video ads on the internet are transformative.

Another contrasting feature of bump in comparison to traditional style TV advertising is that it uses a narrative storytelling style. By framing the advertisement as a story, the appeal widens to a greater range of people, whether in the market to purchase the product or not. With transformational story style advertising, there's less chance of generating resentment from jaded consumers who would rather avoid *yet another* advertisement.

Think about the last time you witnessed a road accident. Probably you couldn't help yourself from looking. Your mind was trying to make sense of what was going on so that you could learn not to make the same dangerous mistake. The scientific reason for why people are attracted to transformational style advertisements rather than informational style advertisements is related to people's desire to make sense of the world around them. There's general acceptance in the academic literature that humans, and probably

Transformational Advertising

An advertisement structure where the viewer experiences the mood, feelings and emotions of the advertisement's story.

other animals with advanced nervous systems, are driven to convert their understanding of the world into stories to help them understand their lives. A story is basically an event that's supported by a beginning that adds context to the event, and an ending that resolves any conflict created by the event. A story has a beginning, middle and an end. If you hear a strange noise at night, it is unlikely that you will be able to sleep again until you find out what the noise was. You'll feel uneasy until you resolve the issue, essentially ending the story. Once you discover that it was only the cat climbing through the window, the story is complete, and you can get back to sleep.

Consider the shampoo ad example given earlier. If the facts about the product are given, such as ingredients, features and price, the consumer will evaluate each fact, making arguments for why the product might or might not be a good fit for them. If the advertisement is not relevant to them because they are not in the market to buy, they'll likely reach the conclusion that the product is unsuitable, and skip the ad. But if the advertisement is presented in a transformational type way, perhaps with a story of how the girl got more compliments at work and felt more alive after using the shampoo, then it forces the viewer to imagine themselves using the product. When you engage someone's imagination, then you can access their memories and emotions, and make them *feel* the advertisement, rather than argue against it. This is transformational advertising.

The power of storytelling in affecting people's wellbeing can be seen in the way that clinical psychologists use it to treat patients suffering from mental trauma. Psychologists believe that mental trauma is not just about the events that caused the distress, but how the person dealt with the events afterwards. In other words, how the victim interprets and constructs the story of what happened. Distressful events such as a divorce, or a significant career setback, cause the sufferer to obsessively run through their minds what happened in an attempt to find causes and make sense of it all. The distress is caused from people's inability to find a satisfactory ending to the story, since the facts don't appear to make sense to them. Psychologists in psychotherapy sessions get the sufferer to tell their story, or sometimes write it down, to help them simplify what happened and therefore help them understand.

Transformational storytelling follows a pattern as described in Todorov's narrative framework. The framework has three parts: equilibrium, disruption and resolution. A story begins with equilibrium where everything is normal and as it should be. Then an event happens, usually some kind of disruption that shakes things up and is out of the ordinary. The story then concludes with a resolution to fix the disruption to bring things back to normal. Most movies follow this script, and it's also found in music videos and even songs. It's the basis of storytelling.

Let's see how one of my favourite movies of all time uses the framework: *Good Will Hunting* (1997).

The film begins with Will (Matt Damon) and Chuckie (Ben Affleck) sitting in a bar talking with friends, having a laugh. The scenes change to shots of the city of Boston, and people going about their daily lives. Then back to Will and Chuckie going for a drive. Then to an MIT classroom, packed full of students, where Professor Lambeau (Stellan Skarsgård) is lecturing. There is equilibrium: all is as it should be, and things are normal and calm.

Things start getting interesting when Professor Lambeau leaves an extremely difficult maths problem on the blackboard overnight, and finds the next morning that someone from outside his classroom has solved it. It turns out that Will, who is actually the janitor, was the person who solved it. Will had a troubled childhood, and following a chain of events lands in trouble with the law. This is the disruption. Will's life is suddenly in chaos.

Professor Lambeau then tries to restore equilibrium by arranging for Will to forego jail time in return for doing psychotherapy with his friend Dr Sean Maguire (Robin Williams). Eventually Will changes his ways, and sets forth into the sunset to 'go see about a girl' he fell in love with. Calm is restored – this is the resolution.

Not surprisingly, this story structure also fits the Nike 'Ronaldinho' advertisement. The scene begins with Ronaldinho sitting calmly on the grass putting his boots on. In the background the stadium is empty, and other team members jog and pass the ball in practice. This is the equilibrium.

Then Ronaldinho stands up, flicks the ball into action with his feet, and begins doing his tricks. The skills escalate rapidly as he begins to kick the ball at the goal crossbar, bouncing it back and kicking it again while not letting the ball touch the ground. The viewer is psychologically aroused and amazed. This is the disruption.

Finally, Ronaldinho's tricks begin to wind down, and he dribbles the ball back to the man who gave him the shoes. He shakes the man's hand, and things return back to normal. Equilibrium is restored – this is the resolution.

These are just two examples, but you will find that almost all of the supervirals discussed in this book follow this basic pattern of storytelling. It should be the starting point for all viral advertising projects.

How to include a brand

Thales Teixeira and his colleagues at Harvard University conducted a study to answer one of the biggest questions faced by advertisers: how should the brand be incorporated into the advertisement (Teixeira *et al.*, 2012)? The reason why this question is so important is because of a double-edged sword in advertising: include the brand too prominently and people will stop taking notice or skip through it. But include the brand too briefly, and people will remember the advertisement, but not the brand. The challenge has always been to find the sweet spot – the middle ground where the advertisement keeps viewers engaged without putting them off, but at the same time makes people remember what the brand was.

What Teixeira and his colleagues found was that the optimal way to include a brand in an advertisement is to 'pulse' it. This means that the brand reveals itself *briefly and intermittently* through the advertisement, rather than just once at the beginning or end. Consider a car advertisement – the new car travels swiftly down a winding road past picturesque scenery. The footage shoots between the driver enjoying the driving experience, and shots of the car from a distance. In between these shots, short glimpses of the steering–wheel or bonnet logo are shown. With this type of pulsed brand placement, people were 10 per cent less likely to skip the advertisement than if the brand were only shown one time at either the beginning or the end.

Tip

Include your brand briefly and intermittently throughout your video rather than predominantly at the beginning or at the end, to minimise the chances of viewers tuning out.

Teixeira's study highlights an important issue that you should spend considerable effort addressing: there's a tendency for people to switch off and not share when they realise they're watching an ad. According to a study done by Charles Adams in the 1960s (Adams, 1965), the average person back then was exposed to around 560 advertisements a day, yet on average only noticed 76. More recent studies in modern times have found similar results (*Media Matters*, 2007). People have been conditioned over many years of advertising exposure to block it out. Your challenge is not only to motivate them to watch, but to affect them in such a way that they are thankful that they watched.

To get through to consumers, marketers realised early on that they had to rethink how internet advertising was produced. Most viral movies, even to this day, are what we call 'user-generated content', which is usually someone's shaky phone footage that has captured something of interest like a road accident, or skateboard trick, or pet cat. Marketers used user-generated content as a starting point, to see if they could use the same structure for advertisements. Early attempts at producing bumps attempted to replicate user-generated content by hiding the brand in some way.

Some of these ads used deception to trick the viewer that it was user generated and not brand generated. An advertisement designed to create buzz for the upcoming movie *The Wackness* (**https://youtu.be/3fdVQSv-SjQ**) was one of the first. The movie begins by showing shaky mobile phone footage of London's Buckingham Palace at night. The URL kingtag.com is displayed on the lower left of the screen, suggesting that perhaps the movie might be from some underground organisation. A man appears wearing a hoody. He's with his friend who is the one taking the phone footage. The scene switches back to the palace to show guards marching past. As soon as the guards are gone, one of the men scales the palace fence, and runs over to the front of the palace where they take cover in the shadows. He produces a spray can and begins writing some graffiti on the front of the palace. The man then escapes back over the palace fence before the guards return. The final shot shows the product of their efforts – the graffiti tag. In stylised graffiti style writing, the tag says 'The Wackness'.

The stunt was counting on controversy to drive the viral effect. But it was also deceptive pretending to be user generated and not professionally produced. They were hoping that people would be curious about what the man had written, and subsequently search the internet to find out what 'The Wackness' meant. An accompanying website was set up to show trailers and other information about the movie. The movie did create some buzz, but never really went viral as the producers intended. It has just 11,000 views on YouTube.

The main reason why this ad failed is because it's deceptive. By displaying the fake URL kingtag.com throughout the whole movie, there was an admission that the ad was fake, and it was easy to find out it was a fake. News quickly spread through the internet that the prank was staged. When viewers discovered the prank was not real, they felt cheated, and this destroyed any chance of it being shared.

Tip

Don't use deception to trick the viewer that your advertisement is user generated and not sponsored by a brand.

Marc 'Eckō' Milecofsky tried a similar prank to generate buzz surrounding his clothing brand Eckō Unltd (**https://youtu.be/ePOiSJQLfJ4**). The movie showed footage of him scaling an airport fence to write some graffiti on the side of the President's Air Force One. What actually happened was that he rented a Boeing 747 and painted one side to look like Air Force One, then spray-painted 'Still Free' on one of the engines. The prank included a website StillFree.com that had more information about the prank. This prank earned 800,000 views, and did significantly better than *The Wackness* ad. The main reason this strategy worked better was that the video was not trying to deceive viewers that it was not an advertisement, but rather the deception was the prank. In addition, the brand was already well known, and the prank fit synergistically with the brand's hip-hop graffiti image.

Rather than deceiving the viewer that your ad is not an ad, a better strategy is to include the brand as a character in the story. According to research done by Vladimir Propp in the nineteenth century, there are six types of character in a story:

1   **Hero (protagonist).** The main character that seeks to do something admirable.

2   **Villain (antagonist).** Tries to inflict evil on the hero.

3   **Donor.** An entity who gives the hero some magic.

4   **Dispatcher.** Character who sends the hero forth to begin their admirable quest.

5   **False hero.** Character who initially appears to be on the side of the hero, but turns out to be against the hero or deceives the hero in some way.

6   **Helper.** Character who helps the hero to restore equilibrium. Like a sidekick.

Successful video advertisements always include at least one of these characters. In the Nike ad, Ronaldinho is the hero. The man who gives Ronaldinho the new football boots is the Dispatcher. But, importantly, the brand is also a character – Nike plays the Donor by providing the 'magic' boots that help Ronaldinho do amazing tricks.

Relying on deception is inferior to including the brand as a character element in a story. In 'The Wackness' and 'Air Force One' ads, the brands don't play meaningful character roles, and therefore are not sufficiently incorporated into the story.

A superviral that included the brand as a character element is the 'LG meteor prank' (**https://youtu.be/Uorrl64vloQ**). The ad begins by showing two men carrying an LG Ultra HD TV in a box. They take the TV to an office, unpack it, and place it behind a desk in place of the window. With a city scape showing, the Ultra HD resolution of the TV is able to display images so clearly that it looks like it's an actual window.

The men then get busy installing hidden cameras around the office.

The prank involves conducting a number of fake job interviews with people who have applied to work in the company. The interviewer is in on the prank. Each candidate walks into the office, and the interviewer introduces himself and asks the candidate to take a seat. On the TV a view of the city is displayed, replicating what you would expect to see outside of any office window. The LG Ultra HD TV is able to render images so clearly that the view from the 'window' looks real.

Then the fun begins. As each candidate is being interviewed, a giant comet rumbles into view from the sky outside the window (actually faked on the TV). The comet is so huge that it looks like it will destroy the city outside. The candidates stand up in panic, pointing at the comet in disbelief and fruitlessly seeking cover behind anything they can find. The interviewer plays along. The comet impacts with a giant explosion and the lights go dark. The candidate fumbles around in the dark before the lights go back on. Then the producers emerge from the hallway to let the candidate in on the prank.

The 'LG meteor prank' is not only clever; it's also a great example of how to include a brand into an advertisement. Like the Nike ad, the LG brand takes a donor character role, providing the magic that makes the whole prank work. The way to make a brand a character in a bump is to include the benefits of the brand into the storyline, not the features.

Punchy bursts

Think about a funny stand-up comic. One thing successful comedians are extremely good at doing is rolling with the jokes, one after the other. They know that as soon as you start telling long stories people lose interest and you're going to die on stage, so they keep their gags short and punchy.

There's a very good reason why comedians roll with short punchy jokes. The impact of any single joke wears off quickly, so they need to hit their audience with another joke soon after to keep the audience engaged.

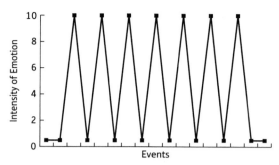

Figure 9.1 Spikes of emotion in a video ad to maximise engagement

Imagine if the bursts of crowd laughter at a comedy gig were plotted onto a line graph. It would look spikey, with each spike representing one burst of laughter. The number of laughter spikes should correspond to the number of jokes told. The number of spikes is a good indication of how successful the show was.

It's the same with viral movies. The aim is to produce as many 'spikes' of emotion in as short a time period as possible. It keeps people engaged. If there's too big a gap between the spikes, people will switch off, and the ad will never get shared. Just like a comedian, to keep people's attention the emotions must roll one after the other in short succession to keep the viewer engaged.

The number of spikes of emotion in a bump-style ad is much greater than a traditional TV-style advertisement. The traditional TV ad structure usually builds up to an epiphany or punchline over time. Frequently, there is just one spike of emotion at the end, if at all.

Bumps in contrast follow a specific pattern, aimed at maximising the number of emotional spikes. The easiest and most common technique used to spike emotions is to edit the movie so that it shows a series of short scenes stitched together, with each scene designed to evoke an emotional response that collectively tells the story.

The 'LG meteor prank' uses this technique. The movie is two minutes long. The 'set-up' of the prank scene takes less than 30 seconds. Once this is over the movie then shows all the job candidates collectively at key stages of the movie, rather than show each candidate's experience individually from initial introduction through to the end of the prank. For example, the beginning of the prank shows each of the four job candidates as they walk through the door and introduce themselves, one after the other. The next key stage of the movie is the actual interview. In ten seconds each of the four candidates is shown being interviewed. The next key stage is the actual prank. From a different camera angle the movie shows the reactions of each of the candidates as the comet appears on the TV. This takes just 30 seconds. The final scene shows the candidates being let in on the prank. The technique of editing the movie down to a series of short bursts of key scenes is known as 'chunking'. The entire movie is edited down to a series of one- to three-second shots, and each candidate's experience is chunked together into the key scenes. By doing this, the movie is able to keep the story punchy with short bursts of humour at the predicament of each of the poor candidates.

This chunking technique was also used by Carlsberg in the superviral 'Stunts with bikers in cinema' ad (**https://youtu.be/RS3iB47nQ6E**) with over one million shares. The advertisement begins with hidden camera shots of people buying movie tickets. The footage then changes to people who have already purchased tickets and have taken their seats. But the movie-goers seated are not your typical movie-goers – they're big burly men covered in tattoos, sitting menacingly with mean looks on their faces. It's clearly a very intimidating crowd, and there are only two seats left in the whole movie theatre – right in the middle of them. Movie-goers who want to claim these last seats have to squeeze past a line of intimidating men, and sit next to a couple of brutes who look like they're having a bad day.

The fun begins when ordinary couples enter the theatre to claim a seat. The entrance to the theatre is at the bottom, and the couples must stand in front of the angry audience to find where their seat is.

The advertisement is edited to capture only the reactions of the couples who enter the movie theatre. Each couple entering the theatre is a mini story, with each story delivering a punch of humour. Some couples turn around and walk out, while other couples just stand there wondering what to do. Some brave couples gingerly step over the intimidating men to take their seats. It leaves the viewer wondering what they would have done.

The end scene shows what happens to the brave couples who take the seats. They're rewarded with cheers from the men, who pass them a Carlsberg beer. Similar to the 'LG meteor prank', the movie uses chunking with scenes that are just seconds long, and all victims of the prank shown back-to-back in the same chunk.

Hook, line and sinker

Often when I'm trying to troubleshoot something by doing an internet search, I come across YouTube movies in the search results that claim to have a solution. The problem is, most of the time I'd prefer to see listed written instructions on a webpage, not a movie, since I don't have enough patience to watch a movie. When it's written instructions I feel more in control over what information I take in, and whether or not the information is suitable. With YouTube movies, I often find I have to wait for the instructor to get to the point, or at least I have a fear that I'll have to wait. In a worst case scenario I'll waste five minutes of my life, which seems like a lot. Ideally I'd like the YouTube person to just tell me how to fix my problem in one sentence, without the introduction, background, lead-up, pictures of their cat . . . But I fear this will never happen.

You've probably heard it before – time is people's most precious asset. For this reason, as soon as people start watching video movies the first thing they do is evaluate how worthwhile the movie is to watch in return for their precious time. If it looks as though the movie might be irrelevant or boring, people don't stand for it and they stop watching. The movie has to impress within the first few seconds, or you've lost them.

The secret to keeping people engaged and halt their thoughts of skipping your beautiful ad is to hook them in. The best way to hook people in is to spike them with an emotion early on. Make them feel something so they stay engaged.

But it's not always easy to spike an emotion early in a movie, because the story structure must begin with a state of equilibrium, as discussed earlier in this chapter. The equilibrium at the beginning of a story sets the scene and provides the necessary context so that the viewer can understand the story later on. It's difficult to add any emotion when things are calm, as the equilibrium stage usually is.

But there is a way – create anticipation. I discuss the power of anticipation in **Chapter 4,** but for now I want to focus on two elements that are particularly effective for hooking the viewer in and keeping their attention in the opening stages. These are 'suspense' and 'intrigue'.

Suspense is an expectation that something important is about to happen, and intrigue is a heightened state of fascination or curiosity. Both focus the viewers' attention, and drive them to want more information. This keeps them watching until you can release some spikes of emotion and make the movie memorable and shareable.

Several of the movies discussed already in this chapter use suspense or intrigue early in the movie to hook the viewer in. The Volkswagen 'Eyes on the road' (**https://youtu.be/R22WNkYKeo8**) superviral, with 800,000 shares is another example. The movie begins with hidden camera footage of movie-goers taking their seats in a theatre. The quality and angle of the footage makes the viewer wonder why movie-goers are being secretly filmed. The footage then switches to a strange looking electronics device being set up in a dark room. Then, the scene switches back to the movie-goers who are by now seated and watching advertisements while waiting for the feature film to start. The advertisement being shown in the theatre is a car advertisement that puts the viewer in the driver's seat, simulating what it would be like to drive the car.

Then the footage returns to the mystery device shown earlier. It is being operated by men sitting in a dark room, and it becomes apparent the device is some kind of transmitter. The men switch the device on, and configure some switches. The footage switches back to the audience watching the car ad, where suddenly, some of their phones begin to buzz. The pranksters in the dark room have used their device to send fake messages to the people who have Bluetooth enabled on their phones. The movie-goers fumble in their pockets to locate their phones, and begin to read the message sent to them. While they are looking at their phones, the driver of the car in the advertisement unexpectedly veers off the road and crashes head-on into a tree. A message on the screen reminds the audience that mobile use is now the leading cause of death behind the wheel.

Creating a strong emotional response requires a movie to immerse the viewer. The only way to do this is to hook the viewer in early. Effective storytelling however relies on an equilibrium stage where the options for introducing emotions are limited. One exception to this restriction is to introduce suspense or intrigue. The Volkswagen 'Eyes on the road' super-viral was successful at keeping the viewer engaged from the beginning, by keeping the viewer intrigued over what was about to happen. The suspense created was spiked with further emotions including a shock reaction and possibly remorse and guilt by those viewers who touch their phones while driving.

Non-linear time scenes

When stories have linear time scenes, they progress from the beginning to the end, just like how time progresses in real life. *Non*-linear time scenes however progress in a non-standard order, like when a story has a flashback, or glimpse into the future before returning to the present.

Many of the video ads discussed in this chapter have non-linear time scenes. But you should be careful if mixing up time sequences in advertisements that you don't create unnecessary confusion for the viewer. Generally people make better sense out of a linear scene structure than a non-linear structure. Consider the movie *Memento* (2000), which jumps from the future to the past to the present, and back to the future again with confusing regularity. The story is further shaken up by a hero who has amnesia. This kind of structure might have some attraction to movie-goers, but for advertising there's no room for challenging people to make sense of what's going on. The more complicated an ad, the less likely it is that someone will share it. If it isn't effortless to watch, people will give up.

Non-linear time sequences can be useful however for increasing the impact of a video ad by moving the story along quicker, and hooking the viewer in early. In general, Todorov's narrative framework, discussed earlier in this chapter, should always take priority over decisions to use non-linear time scenes. Or another way to think about this, non-linear time scenes should be used to ensure your video ad adheres to Todorov's narrative framework.

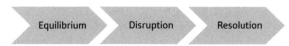

Figure 9.2 Todorov's narrative framework

Consider the superviral 'Pepsi's Jeff Gordon test drive' (**https://youtu.be/ Q5mHPo2yDG8**) with 2.7 million shares. The ad features stock car driver Jeff Gordon who visits a car dealer in disguise to test drive one of their Chevy Camaros. The story begins with Jeff just beginning his test drive, with the car dealer sitting next to him. Consistent with Todorov's framework everything is in equilibrium, just a normal test drive at a typical car dealership. The movie quickly shifts to the disruption stage when the customer starts driving erratically. Things escalate when the driver starts doing doughnuts, and the car dealer has no idea what's going on and begins to freak out.

It's at this point that the movie goes back in time (non-linear time sequence) to help the viewer understand what's going on. The time-in-the-past scene is in a makeup room, where the viewer learns that the customer is actually Jeff Gordon in disguise. The scene shows Jeff getting disguised, followed by him browsing the car lot and being approached by the car dealer. Of course car dealers are always very keen to get potential customers interested in a car so they can progress the sale. Jeff shows interest in the Camero, and the car dealer convinces Jeff to take the next step and test drive it.

The movie then jumps back to the disruption stage of the movie where Jeff proceeds to scare the daylights out of the car dealer by driving like a rally driver on tarmac. After the dramatic ride, the car dealer and Jeff exit the car, and Jeff discloses the prank to the dealer, providing the resolution to the prank.

The 'Pepsi's Jeff Gordon test drive' illustrates a very important point about changing the order of the time sequence. It adds to the punch of the movie by hooking people in earlier, and creating suspense and intrigue. If the ad was linear, progressing from the makeup room to the car dealership to the driving, the equilibrium stage at the beginning would have been too long and people would have tuned out. By including the flashback in a non-linear sequence, the movie is able to hook the viewer in early.

> ## Tip
>
> If you're going to change the time sequence, make sure the narrative sequence from equilibrium to resolution is not affected. Otherwise you'll end up with an overly confusing ad that people don't understand and won't share.

The structure of advertisements has changed dramatically since marketers discovered the concept of viral advertising. It's no longer enough just to get noticed – viewers expect something in return for their valuable time taken to watch your ad. Trading value is the key to a successful bump, and affecting the viewer in a positive way is the only way to deliver that value.

Action plan for bump

Incorporating a brand into a highly shareable video is challenging. Consumers are conditioned to switch off when they detect an advertisement, and your carefully planned efforts to make a video shareable can be jeopardised if people don't feel like they're getting some value in return for watching. A video ad designed for sharing on the internet requires a different structure than the traditional made-for-TV style of ad. The bump style of advertising addresses these issues.

To create a bump style advertisement, several elements are necessary:

1   **Create a story.** A transformative advertising structure with a strong story is required to create the spikes of emotion needed to capture and hold the viewer's attention. People are attracted to stories, and a story is needed to transfer value to the viewer in the form of entertainment and satisfaction. Use a narrative framework to tell the story. Start with an equilibrium phase, introduce a disruption, and always complete the story with a resolution.

2   **Include the brand.** Decide on an option to include your brand: either (1) the brand reveals itself briefly and intermittently through the advertisement, or (2) the brand is included as a character in the story. The preferred option is the latter (to include the brand as a character in the story). It's more subtle than dedicating explicit scenes in the video to showcasing the brand, however brief. Including the brand as a character also has many more options to add associations to the brand based on the role that the brand character plays. The options to include the brand as a character include: hero (protagonist), donor or helper. If including the brand as the hero is chosen, the brand plays a main role in the story. The disadvantage of doing this is that it can create a problem with the brand

▶

taking an overly prominent role. The chances of the viewer concluding the video is a brand-sponsored TV advertisement are increased if the brand is too prominent, and therefore there is more chance of them switching off. Placing the brand as the helper is another option, where the brand helps to resolve the conflict somehow. This model is typically used by advertisers to demonstrate how a product is able to resolve a consumer problem. A shampoo ad might demonstrate how the shampoo is able to control the problem of dandruff. The best of these three options is to include the brand as the donor character. The donor character is the entity that gives the hero of the story some magic to help them achieve their goals. The Nike 'Ronaldinho' and 'LG meteor prank' video ads are two examples described in this chapter where the brand gives the main character or storyline magic. This ties the movie together and creates intrigue. When the brand is central to the story in terms of enabling the entertainment (by providing the magic), viewers are more likely to extract value from the experience, and form favourable associations towards the brand. Whichever strategy is chosen, you should take care to focus on the benefits of using the product, not the physical attributes of the product. People tend to think about how brands solve problems, and the benefits of using the brand, rather than the physical attributes of the product itself.

3 **Structure emotion.** The structure of your video movie should spike hits of emotion. The spiking should begin early in the story to hook people in and maximise engagement. Decisions on the structure of emotional spikes should be made before the script is drafted, and before storyboarding begins. After a script has been produced, the spikes should be fine-tuned. Using the storyboard, mark out where the spikes of emotion are likely to occur, so you can visualise the emotional ups of the viewing experience. Then try to estimate the time between each spike. The aim is to shorten as much as possible the time periods between each spike of emotion. Ideally you want as many spikes as possible, as close together as possible. You might consider using a non-linear time scene structure to engage the user early with a spike of emotion, especially if your chosen story has a long equilibrium phase before the disruption stage. This might be necessary for some story types, especially since creating a spike in emotion in the equilibrium phase is relatively difficult in comparison to the disruption phase.

4   **Use chunking.** It is important that the story structure is simple and effortless to watch. People expect a story to follow a predefined pattern from past to present to future. Jumping around short scenes creates confusion for viewers too easily. One way to simplify the story structure while at the same time spike emotions is to use chunking. This involves grouping common elements together to ensure a smooth linear transition from the equilibrium scenes, through the disruption scenes, and finally to the resolution scenes. The 'LG meteor prank' uses chunking by showing all actor scenes in the equilibrium phase one after the other in short bursts. Then the disruption scenes are all shown in chunks one after the other, and finally all the resolution scenes. The result is that each element within a chunk is able to deliver a spike of emotion, resulting in multiple spikes of emotion at each stage, while retaining a simplified linear story structure.

Conclusion

Jerry had a small butcher's shop near Swansea in the southern part of Wales. On the outside of his shop was written 'High quality purveyors of meat and poultry since 1869'. Jerry's father and his father before him were butchers, and to this day Jerry is proud to still sell meat that had been reared on his family's farm.

Like many butchers in these modern times, Jerry's business had suffered from a consumer trend towards buying meat from the large chain super-markets. Jerry also suspected there were more vegans and vegetarians than there used to be, and graffiti attacks on his shop by animal rights protes-tors seemed to have increased in recent years. If it weren't for his most loyal customers, Jerry suspected he might have gone out of business years earlier. The reason why Jerry's shop had survived was because he had built a reputa-tion for providing high quality cuts of meat, and everyone knew that Jerry would give them the best advice on what meat was best for any occasion. People tended to come to Jerry for his advice just as much as his meat.

Jerry's shop was traditional, and so was he. Of course he had heard about the internet and social media, and he was even curious, but Jerry wasn't really a computer user. He got frustrated too easily, and he would ask his wife Mabel to take care of it. One Christmas when his extended family came together for the midday feast, he asked his teenage niece Luci to please teach him about social media. Luci got her phone out, and pulled up her Facebook account. 'See Uncle Jerry? This is called Facebook. People share things on it'. Jerry looked puzzled. 'Share things? What types of things?' Luci raised her eyebrows and looked at Jerry like he was an adorable panda. 'Well . . . People share photos mostly. Anything that makes other people smile. When I shared that funny photo of us on holiday last summer, people on Facebook clicked this 'Like' button, and some people clicked this 'Share' button. It made me feel good that people liked it'. Jerry thought about it for a while. 'So if I have a picture that people like, they'll share it with others?' 'Yes!' said Luci. 'Just don't share that one of you with your shirt off when we went to the beach!'

Jerry thought about his niece's lesson on social media for the rest of the holiday. He wondered what he could share on 'the Facebook thing' that others would like and share. By the end of the holiday, he had an idea. Jerry put a lot of work into his hand reared herd of cattle, and he took pride in cutting each steak to perfection. One of the things that Jerry was most annoyed about as a butcher was people who wasted his high quality cuts of meat by not cooking them properly. The perfect steak was rare, juicy and tender-seared but red 75 per cent through the centre. Once you tasted Jerry's perfect steak, the experience was unforgettable! He couldn't stand the thought of someone wasting his precious meat by not cooking it properly. He decided to make instructions on how to cook the perfect steak, and compare it to how steak shouldn't be cooked. Surely people wanted to know how to cook the perfect steak he thought. That would be shareable.

He took some meat home that evening and cut six equally sized steaks. He cooked the first one 'well done' – 100 per cent brown all the way through. A complete waste of meat – the result is tough and tasteless. He cooked the next steak 'medium well'. Again, according to Jerry, also a waste of good meat. The next he cooked 'medium', with 25 per cent of the meat still pink inside. Although palatable, still not ideal. The next he cooked 'medium rare' – seared with 50 per cent red centre, just passed the point of being the perfect steak. He then cooked the perfect steak – red 75 per cent through the centre, juices flowing, and tender to the point of melting in the mouth. Finally, for comparison's sakes, he cooked a so-called 'blue rare' steak – seared on the outside, completely red throughout, undercooked and difficult to chew with a gel like texture. He cut each steak in half, and took a side picture of each to clearly show how much red each one still had through the middle. With Luci's help, he compiled all the pictures into one image, with a description beneath each. He then asked Luci to help him setup a Facebook page for his butchery, and uploaded his photo. Since Jerry didn't have any followers on his new Facebook page yet, Luci recommended to post the image on someone else's page that already had a lot of followers. A quick search on Facebook using the word 'meat' found an active discussion page for meat lovers versus vegans. Perfect! This should be interesting he thought to himself. Luci posted the image for him with the comment: 'You've been cooking steak the wrong way'.

The next morning Jerry checked the Facebook group to see if anyone had liked his image. To his delight, it had 630 Likes, and 87 Shares. Jerry had no idea if that was a lot or not, but he was grinning from ear to ear. Luci was right, it does feel good to be liked on Facebook.

Over the course of the next couple of weeks, Jerry's image eventually found its way onto the social image site Pinterest where it really took off, earning 25,000 Repins, and 3000 Likes. It was one of the most popular images on Pinterest that month, and Jerry became a local celebrity as word got around of his 'You've been cooking steak the wrong way' campaign. Jerry became known as 'that steak guy', which to Jerry was an honour, since all he really wanted to do was stop the world from ruining steak.

Jerry wasn't an expert at social media, but like many of the characters in this book, he followed his intuition on human nature and the value people place on the sharing of information. Jack (**Chapter 5**) came close to losing his motorcycle business, until he figured out that people care about how he makes them feel, before they care about what he sells. Trevor with his flower shop (**Chapter 3**) discovered that people's behaviour is decided by their emotions. Jerry and the other characters in this book are not C-level marketers, nor do they have fancy degrees. They don't have large marketing budgets, nor do they have a staff of many. They're regular people, who figured out how to affect people, not just get noticed. That is the first lesson when going viral – people will share when they care deeply. It's not enough to be interesting or noticeable, you have to evoke an emotional response. You have to affect people in a meaningful way.

Jerry's picture became popular after he posted it on a Facebook page with vegans and meat eaters. In his 30 years as a butcher he was no stranger to the rants and attacks from anti-meat-eater extremists. But Jerry wasn't out for revenge, he simply wanted to share something with the world that *he* thought was important. He wanted to show the world how to cook steak, but his intuition told him that he had to join an argument for people to share, because people have to care. Of course most of the comments on Jerry's Facebook post were from opposing sides arguing their case for or against what Jerry had contributed. Just like Grace (**Chapter 8**) and her over-exposed blue-and-black or white-and-gold dress picture that swept the world, Jerry learned that people feel comfortable about their lives when they can rationalise their situation. This is the next lesson about going viral, when seeding shareable content, people will rationalise their membership to a group when their beliefs can't be easily changed, and as a result they'll defend what's important to them. This creates the initial 'buzz' that's required for successful seeding, and ultimately the viral spread.

In the nine chapters of this book I've covered several inspirational stories like Jerry's. Jack taught us the importance of helping other people to live their dreams, Trevor taught us how following your emotions leads to happiness, Ernő Rubik taught us how opportunity comes from perseverance, and Chris Rock taught us about perseverance in times of adversity. What they each have in common is contagious passion. By investing their time to create something shareable they earned something larger than the self. What they got back from their efforts was meaning and fulfilment. Each of their stories holds an important lesson to help us understand the secrets of going viral.

When we think about things going viral on the internet, we assume that it must be a function of randomness. And we have this simplistic view that although some marketers are very clever at making advertisements, the ones that went viral got lucky somehow. At the same time, we marvel at all kinds of strange behaviours in the world, which suggest that people behave in predictable ways. In this book I have put the microscope on people's propensity to share. When ideas catch on, it shouldn't be a surprise. You only have to peer under the hood to solve the puzzle. In the words of Ernő Rubik: 'The problems of puzzles are very near the problems of life. Like life's journey to find meaning and happiness, the secret to share is understanding how people care'.

Bibliography

Adams, C.F. (1965) *Common Sense in Advertising*, New York: McGraw-Hill.

Berger, J. (2014) 'Word of mouth and interpersonal communication: A review and directions for future research', *The Journal of Consumer Psychology*, 24(4), 586–607.

Cabral, L. and Hortaçsu, A. (2010) 'The dynamics of seller reputation: theory and evidence from eBay', *The Journal of Industrial Economics*, 58 (March): 54–78.

Earp, S.E. and Maney, D.L. (2012) 'Birdsong: is it music to their ears?' *Frontiers in Evolutionary Neuroscience*, 28.

Ekman, P., *et al.* (1992) 'Facial expressions of emotion: an old controversy and new findings', *Philosophical Transactions of the Royal Society*, (B335): 63–69.

Gabrielsson, A. and Lindström, E. (2001) 'The influence of musical structure on emotional expression'. In Juslin, P. N. and Sloboda, J. A. (eds), *Music and Emotion: Theory and Research*, 223–243. New York: Oxford University Press.

Laurin, K., Kille, D.R. and Eibach, R.P. (2013) '"The way I am is the way you ought to be": perceiving one's relational status as unchangeable motivates normative idealization of that status', *Psychological Science*, 24(8): 1523–1532.

Luca, M. (2011) 'Reviews, reputation, and revenue: the case of Yelp.com', *Harvard Business School Working Paper*, 12-016 (September).

Media Matters (2007) 'Our rising ad dosage: it's not as oppressive as some think', 15 February.

Opinion Matters (2011) 'Little White Lies'. Available from: **https:// beautifulpeoplecdn.s3.amazonaws.com/studies/usa_studies.pdf**

Rogers, E. (2003) *Diffusion of Innovations*, New York: Simon & Schuster.

Routledge, C., *et al.* (2011) 'The past makes the present meaningful: nostalgia as an existential resource'. *Journal of Personality and Social Psychology*, 101(3): 638–652.

Scherer, K.R. and Zentner, M.R. (2001) 'Emotional effects of music: production rules', In Juslin, P. N. and Sloboda, J. A. (eds), *Music and Emotion: Theory and Research*, 361–392. New York: Oxford University Press.

Sedikides, C., *et al.* (2008) 'Nostalgia: past, present, and future', *Current Directions in Psychological Science*, 17(5): 304–307.

Teixeira, T., Wedel, M. and Pieters, R. (2012) 'Emotion-induced engagement in internet video advertisements', *Journal of Marketing Research*, 49(2): 144–159.

Todorov, T. (1967) *Littérature et Signification*, Paris, Larousse.

Unruly/ Newscorp (2015). Unruly viral video chart. London.

Vandello, J. A., Goldschmied, N. P. and Richards, D. A. R. (2007). 'The appeal of the underdog'. *Personality and Social Psychology Bulletin*, 33(12), 1603–1616.

Young, R., Sweeting, H. and West, P. (2006) 'Prevalence of deliberate self-harm and attempted suicide within contemporary Goth youth subculture: longitudinal cohort study', *British Medical Journal*, 332 (7549): 1058–1061.

Index

Do you want your people to be the very best at what they do?

Talk to us about how we can help.

As the world's leading learning company, we know a lot about what your people need in order to be better at what they do.

Whatever subject or skills you've got in mind (from presenting or persuasion to coaching or communication skills), and at whatever level (from new-starters through to top executives) we can help you deliver tried-and-tested, essential learning straight to your workforce – whatever they need, whenever they need it and wherever they are.

Talk to us today about how we can:

- Complement and support your existing learning and development programmes
- Enhance and augment your people's learning experience
- Match your needs to the best of our content
- Customise, brand and change it to make a better fit
- Deliver cost-effective, great value learning content that's proven to work.

Contact us today:
corporate.enquiries@pearson.com

ALWAYS LEARNING

PEARSON